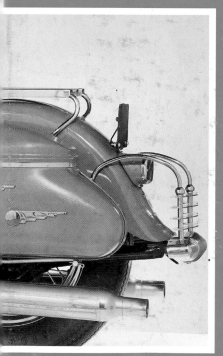

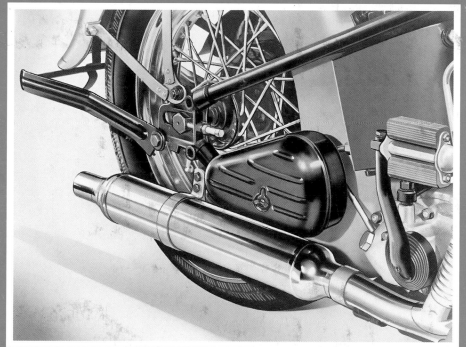

ART OF THE HARLEY-DAVIDSON® MOTORCYCLE

HARLEY-DAVIDSON®

PHOTOGRAPHY BY DAVID BLATTEL WITH TEXT BY DAIN GINGERELLI

motorbooks

First published in 2011 by MBI Publishing Company and Motorbooks, an imprint of MBI Publishing Company, 400 First Avenue North, Suite 300, Minneapolis, MN 55401 USA.

Published under license from Harley-Davidson Motor Company.

The information in this book is true and complete to the best of our knowledge. All recommendations are made without any guarantee on the part of the author or Publisher, who also disclaims any liability incurred in connection with the use of this data or specific details.

We recognize, further, that some words, model names, and designations mentioned herein are the property of the trademark holder. We use them for identification purposes only.

Motorbooks titles are also available at discounts in bulk quantity for industrial or sales-promotional use. For details write to Special Sales Manager at MBI Publishing Company, 400 First Avenue North, Suite 300, Minneapolis, MN 55401 USA.

To find out more about our books, visit us online at www.motorbooks.com.

ISBN-13: 978-0-7603-4130-8

Printed in China
10 9 8 7 6 5 4 3 2 1

Acquisitions Editor: Darwin Holmstrom
Creative Director: Rebecca Pagel
Cover design: Simon Larkin
Book design: Simon Larkin and Christopher Fayers

On the front and back cover (background) and front endpaper:
   2009 FXDFSE CVO Fat Bob
On the title page: 1941 Model FL
Opposite: 1928 Model JDH
On page 189: 1946 Model FL
On page 191: 2011 Dyna Super Glide Custom
On the back cover (from left): 1915 Model 11-F (p12), 1956 Model FL (p49), and 2010 CVO Electra-Glide Ultra Classic (p185)

CONTENTS

CHAPTER SEVEN

FACTORY CUSTOMS:
LOW RIDER AND
WIDE GLIDE MODELS

CHAPTER EIGHT

CIVILIZED CHOPPERS:
THE SOFTAIL MODELS

CHAPTER NINE

SETTING THE RECORD:
THE RACE BIKES

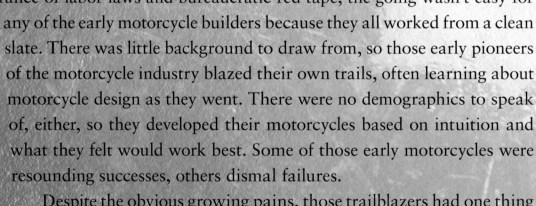

CHAPTER ONE
FINDING FORM:
THE EARLY HARLEY® MOTORCYCLES

The story has been told time and again during the past 100 or so years about the small wooden shed where three young men—William S. Harley, Arthur Davidson and his brother Walter—created the first Harley-Davidson motorcycle. Things were quite different in terms of forming a new business back in 1903, and without interference from governmental regulatory bodies and environmental agencies to shackle their progress, the four men from Milwaukee, Wisconsin, set out to build a business empire that became known as the Harley-Davidson Motor Company.

But even without the hindrance of labor laws and bureaucratic red tape, the going wasn't easy for any of the early motorcycle builders because they all worked from a clean slate. There was little background to draw from, so those early pioneers of the motorcycle industry blazed their own trails, often learning about motorcycle design as they went. There were no demographics to speak of, either, so they developed their motorcycles based on intuition and what they felt would work best. Some of those early motorcycles were resounding successes, others dismal failures.

Despite the obvious growing pains, those trailblazers had one thing in common: they all shared a passion for progress. And that's probably the underlying key to why the motorcycle industry didn't fail more than a century ago and why it continues to flourish to this day.

A similar Model 6 engine.

1910 MODEL 6-A

In 1910 the 4-horsepower, 30-cubic-inch single used new cylinder barrels with more cooling fins. This was the final year for radial cooling fins on the cylinder head. Engineering introduced a belt idler mechanism that allowed the rider to stop the motorcycle without killing the engine. To improve power transmission to the rear wheel, engineering widened the flat leather belt from 1.5 to 1.75 inches. Harley-Davidson manufactured 334 of these motorcycles in 1910, selling them for $250 apiece.

SPECIFICATIONS

Engine Displacement:	30 cubic inches
Price:	$210
Final Drive:	1.75-inch leather belt
Wheelbase:	55 inches

LORE

- Harley manufactured 2,302 examples of the Model 6.
- In 1910, Harley-Davidson motorcycles still retained a total-loss electrical system.

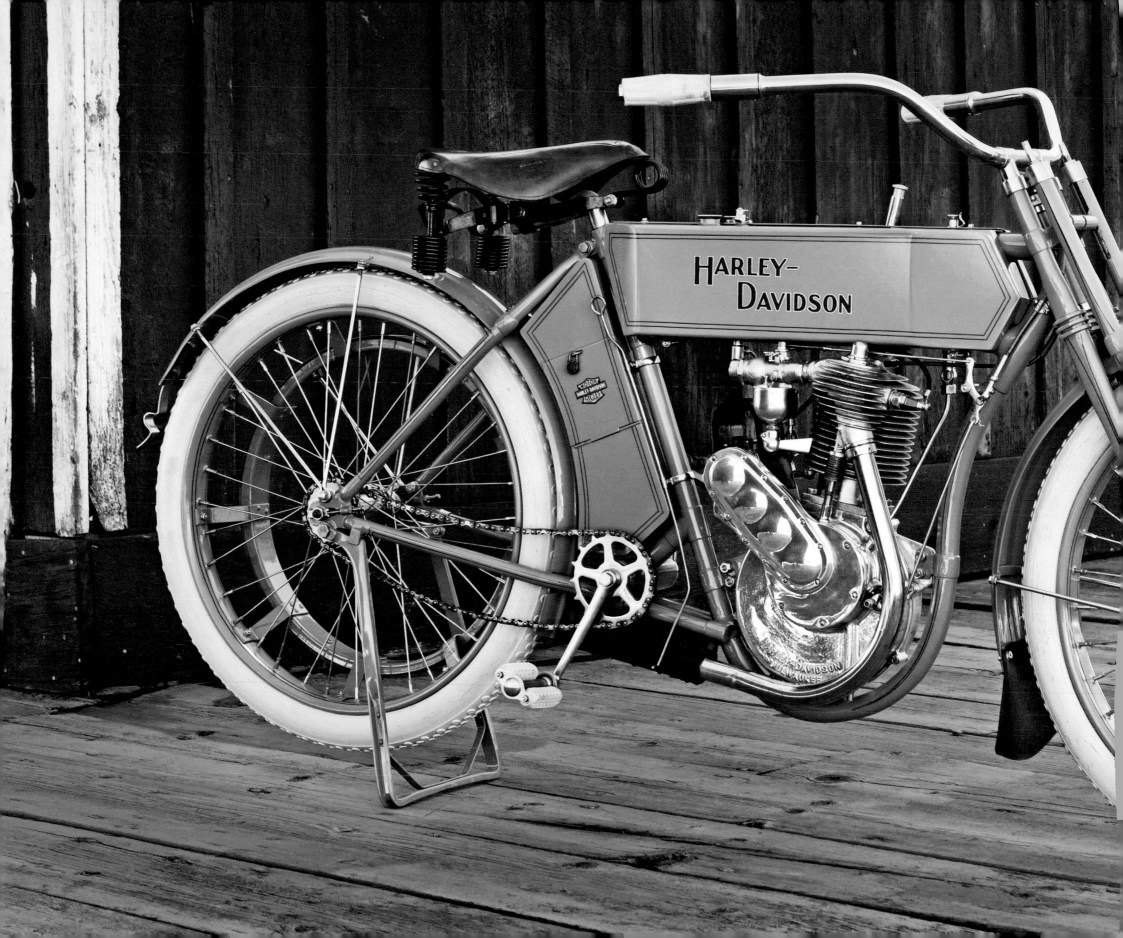

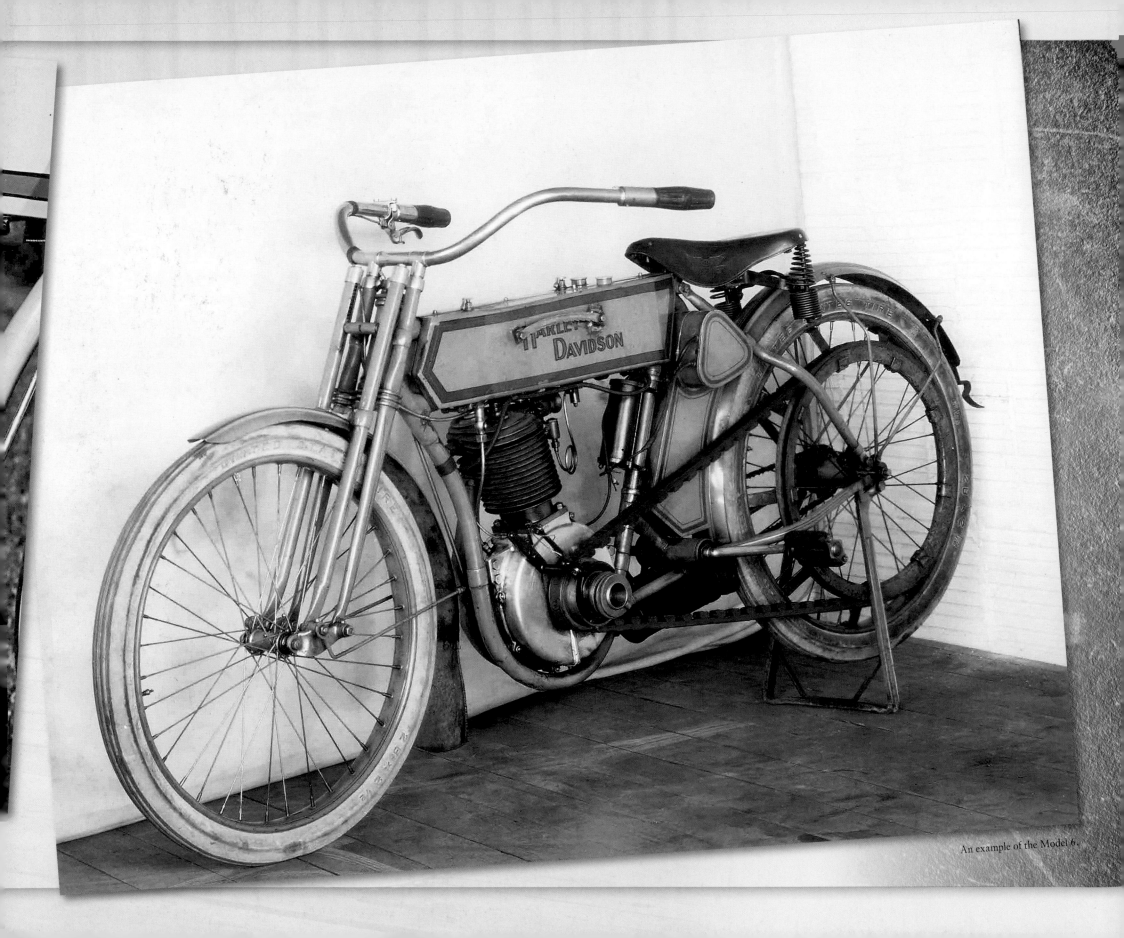

An example of the Model 6.

1911 MODEL 7 SINGLE

In 1911 the V-twin engine returned to Harley-Davidson's lineup. Harley introduced its first V-twin in 1909, but that engine proved a failure so Harley took it off the market, buying back the bikes that had already been sold. The engineering team worked for two years to correct all that was wrong with the V-twin engine. Meanwhile, the tried-and-tested single carried on 1910–1911. The single-cylinder engine, which had earned the nickname Silent Grey Fellow because it was so quiet, remained reliable and popular through the period. For 1911 the inlet-over-exhaust engine was given a new frame that sported a lower seat height for improved rider comfort. Interestingly, low seat height remains high on the list of features requested by Harley customers today.

1915 MODEL 11-F

Like the Model 11-J, the Model 11-F used the upgraded 11-horsepower V-twin engine that Harley-Davidson improved for 1915. The engine had a mechanically driven oil pump for more positive lubrication, a major improvement because it eliminated the need for the rider to work the hand pump that had been required to maintain pressure in the oil tank while riding. The mechanically driven pump did all the work, and did it in a more reliable way. Even though the 11-F's engine had this new feature, the bike qualified as the poor man's Harley of the time because it lacked the new electrical system found on the 11-J. Using the old acetylene-burning lights saved 11-F owners $35 compared to the 11-J's MSRP, a hefty sum in 1915. Obviously the savings was worth it to customers, because the 11-F topped all other Harley models for the year, making it the best-selling Harley up to that time. The new engine also proved popular for racing, and Harley-Davidson offered a race model with the new engine for customers wanting to compete on dirt ovals and board tracks that were popular at the time.

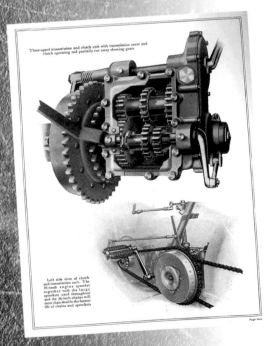

Three-speed transmission and clutch unit with transmission cover and clutch operating rod partially cut away showing gears

Left side view of clutch and transmission unit. The 16-tooth engine sprocket together with the large sprockets used throughout and the 16-inch chains will more than double the former life of chains and sprockets.

Page Nine

SPECIFICATIONS

Engine Displacement:	30 cubic inches
Transmission:	3-speed
Horsepower:	11 horsepower
Wheelbase:	59.5 inches

LORE

- 9,855 11-Fs were sold in 1915.
- Even though the 11-J had electrical lighting, the 11-F still relied on acetylene lamps.

1915 MODEL 11-J WITH SIDECAR

Today we take for granted that all motorcycles have strong and dependable electrical systems that can power lights strong enough to illuminate the road ahead for night riding. But until 1915, Harley-Davidson motorcycles, like most other brands, relied on dim headlamps powered by acetylene gas—if they had lights at all. But these new electrical systems were still optional, and many buyers elected to not order the new-fangled electrical lights. Perhaps they distrusted all the twentieth-century technology that seemed to bombard them at every turn. Still, the Model 11-J had much to offer besides electric lighting. For example, a redesigned engine that relied on improved intake ports and new flywheels boosted power by about 30 percent over previous designs. The result: 11 horsepower, an impressive figure for the time.

SPECIFICATIONS

Engine Displacement:	60 cubic inches
Horsepower:	11 horsepower
Weight:	325 pounds
Wheelbase:	59.5 inches

LORE

- Improved intake ports bumped horsepower from 8 to 11.
- In 1914, one year prior, Harley transmissions had only two speeds by way of a unique two-speed rear hub assembly.

1918 MODEL 18-J

By 1918 Harley-Davidson had gone to a single color, olive drab, which some historians contend was requested by the U.S. military. By 1917 it appeared likely that America was going to be drawn into the Great War in Europe, which meant the U.S. Army was going to need a lot of motorcycles to serve near the front lines, and they'd need them quickly. Using a color that was war-friendly would make the transition from civilian to military use easier. And to prepare customers for the new color, Harley sales literature of the time boasted that the paint made for the most beautiful machine which has ever left the Harley-Davidson factories. "There was no need to justify the Model 18-J itself because it ranked as one of the top mass-produced motorcycles of its time."

SPECIFICATIONS

Engine Displacement:	60 cubic inches
Horsepower:	16 horsepower at 3,000 rpm
Weight:	325 pounds
Wheelbase:	59.5 inches

LORE

- Olive drab remained a standard color for Harleys until 1928.

- Harley-Davidson opened its Quartermaster School in 1917 to train U.S. Army motorcycle mechanics. After the war it was renamed the Service School.

1926 MODEL BA

The 1936 Harley-Davidson Model E—the Knucklehead—had its genesis in an OHV single-cylinder engine design developed 10 years earlier and used in the Model AA and BA. After a 1924 fact-finding trip to Europe, Harley-Davidson's management instructed company engineers to produce a model powered by a single-cylinder, 350-cc (21-cubic-inches) engine. Engineering produced two variations, one using a side-valve head, the other with an overhead-valve arrangement called the Peashooter (originally applied to the racing single) because of the unique pop-pop-pop exhaust sound it made. Both engines offered reliable performance, but American customers still preferred the larger, more powerful twin-cylinder models, so the little singles never really caught on. The affordable singles proved popular in the export market, establishing the Harley-Davidson brand worldwide.

SPECIFICATIONS

Engine Displacement:	21 cubic inches
Horsepower:	10 horsepower at 4,000 rpm
Transmission:	3-speed
Weight:	263 pounds
Wheelbase:	56.5 inches

LORE

- The Model BA single was an overhead-valve design.
- The 1926 singles acquired the nickname Peashooter due to their exhaust sound.

1927 MODEL JDS WITH SIDECAR

Harley-Davidson added sidecars to its line in 1914. And as sidecars grew in popularity, the engineering department began to offer engines tuned specifically for hauling the side-mounted rigs. The early sidecars were built and supplied by the Rogers Company until 1925, at which time Harley-Davidson assumed manufacturing the "chairs" (as some enthusiasts called them) until the end of 2010, when the company announced it was dropping the sidecar from its lineup. Presumably, the popularity of the Tri Glide three-wheeler helped management make the decision to suspend sidecar production after 97 years. In 1927 the Model JDS used a 74-cubic-inch inlet-over-exhaust V-twin engine to help tote its rig. The following year the JD engine was joined in the lineup by the JDH, which had a two-cam bottom end similar to the factory race engine that was so dominant at tracks throughout the 1920s. The standard olive drab paint scheme would remain through the year, too, but for 1928 new—and more interesting—colors would be introduced as options for customers.

SPECIFICATIONS

Engine Displacement	74 cubic inches
Horsepower	24 horsepower
Weight	405 pounds (less sidecar)

LORE

- JDS models had different gear ratios to compensate for the addition of the sidecar.

- Among the names for the sidecar were "chair," "sidehack," and "rig."

1928 MODEL JDH

The JDH was Harley-Davidson's flagship model for 1929. The inlet-over-exhaust engine's new two-cam design was based on the successful race engine that first competed in 1919 and had been dominant throughout the 1920s. And while Harley-Davidson's 1929 models were the first to offer optional paint colors other than the olive drab that had been the standard since 1917, the JDH was to be the final IOE engine that Harley-Davidson would offer. The mainstay IOE engine—even with the new two-cam design—was destined to be replaced by the VL, a model with a flathead engine that eventually proved to be more reliable and more powerful than any Harley model ever before. But in the meantime the JDH and its popular 74-cubic-inch IOE engine, and the JD, which sported a motor displacing 61 cubic inches, were immensely popular at about the same time that the world was heading into the Great Depression. The economic crisis was reflected in sales of new Harley-Davidson motorcycles, too, and by 1930 sales figures had taken a noticeable dip.

SPECIFICATIONS

Engine Displacement:	74 cubic inches
Horsepower:	29 horsepower at 4,000 rpm
Weight:	408 pounds
Wheelbase:	59.5 inches

LORE

- Harley's first two-cam engines were used for racing.
- The first-ever front brake on a Harley-Davidson motorcycle appeared in 1928.

1932 MODEL VL

The new 74-cubic-inch flathead engine that bowed in 1930 was not without controversy. And after customers' engines experienced a rash of mechanical problems, even company president William H. Davidson admitted that the model was launched prematurely, citing a long list of mechanical woes that plagued bikes in early 1930. But as Harley-Davidson had done before in such circumstances, the Milwaukee company stood behind its product, rectifying all that was wrong with the original V and VL engines. Heading the list of improvements for 1931 was a new die-cast Schebler carburetor that had smoother interior surfaces for improved air and fuel flow. And on top of the improvements, a reverse gear was available as an option, intended mainly for sidecar applications. Among the minor fixes were stronger mounting tabs for the chain guard and a new fuel strainer. The fixes were enough to hold over into the 1932 model year, too. And good thing, because the Great Depression held the country in an economic stranglehold, stymieing sales for the duration of the year.

SPECIFICATIONS

Engine Displacement:	74 cubic inches
Transmission:	3-speed with optional reverse
Price:	$320

LORE

- The Model B was brought back for 1932 and sold for only $195.
- To further offset expenses in 1932, Harley-Davidson's four founding fathers took 50 percent pay cuts.

1933 MODEL VLD

With little capital available to make major changes for 1933 models, Harley-Davidson's engineers got creative, introducing a few minor and low-cost improvements for the year. Chief among them was the Ride Control option that consisted of a pair of slotted steel plates mounted on the front fork assembly. By changing the position of the slotted plates, the suspension could be tailored to meet the rider's specific needs. While the Ride Control option didn't alter the bike's handling much, the feature proved popular among customers, as did the Buddy Seat, which was an elongated saddle that made room for a passenger on the back portion. This style seat later became popular with FL owners when the Duo-Glide and early Electra-Glide models became Harley-Davidson's top sellers in the 1950s and 1960s. But perhaps the most welcome feature for 1933 VL customers was the wide selection of paint and graphics that Harley-Davidson offered. And if that wasn't enough, chrome-plated components were added to the list. If for no other reason, 1933 proved to be a watershed year for Harley-Davidson in terms of how the company's marketing team approached the way it viewed its customers' wants and needs.

SPECIFICATIONS

Engine Displacement:	74 cubic inches
Horsepower:	29 horsepower
Weight:	529 pounds

LORE

- A 1933 VLE (higher compression engine) set a world speed record of 104 mph.
- The Great Depression forced Harley-Davidson to run its factory at about 20 percent in 1933.

1934 MODEL VLD

Stylish full-valance fenders graced all 1934 model year Harley-Davidson motorcycles. The VLD, with its art deco graphics, set the standard for eye-catching paint schemes. But the 1934 VLD boasted more than just eye candy, the most notable mechanical upgrade being the new, more efficient intake manifold and carburetor. The combination was good for about a 15 percent power gain. The increased power came with a corresponding increase in the VLD's retail price—customers in 1934 paid $10 more for a VLD than the previous year. In addition, the 74-cubic-inch side-valve engine's flow-through lubrication system received an improved oil pump for better delivery to the internal moving parts. And the magnesium pistons, while lighter in weight, had proven to be unreliable, so they were replaced in 1934 with aluminum slugs. The upgraded engine was given the nickname the "TNT motor" by the company.

SPECIFICATIONS

Engine Displacement:	74 cubic inches
Horsepower:	36 horsepower
Weight:	390 pounds
Price:	$320

LORE

- 1934 was the final year for placing the toolbox under the VLD's headlight.
- Harley-Davidson's 1934 sales were spread over 16 months, not 12 as was customary.

1937 MODEL UL

Starting in 1937 the 74-cubic-inch flathead engine became known as the Model U. The new engine featured roller bearings and stronger components throughout, and a dry sump lubrication system similar to that of the Model E overhead-valve engine. The flathead models also were given frames that were reinforced in key areas. In addition, the big side-valve models (the 74-cubic-inch UL and 80-cubic-inch UH) received styling makeovers that matched what was offered on the overhead-valve E. The valance fenders, streamlined taillight, and art deco graphics made the L-head models look more modern and up to date. No doubt, Harley-Davidson was making a statement to its customers and to its creditors that the company was determined to ride out the Great Depression that had forced lesser companies into bankruptcy.

SPECIFICATIONS

Engine Displacement:	74 cubic inches
Carburetor:	Linkert
Transmission:	4-speed

LORE

- Engines with flow-through lubrication systems earned the nickname "road oilers," and for obvious reasons.
- Many enthusiasts mistakenly think that all U models have 80-inch engines.

1940 MODEL UL

By 1940 the venerable flathead Big Twin engine had been thoroughly sorted out by Harley-Davidson engineers, making it one of the most reliable models of its time. But taking leads from the new overhead-valve Model E and EL, the engineers adapted a dry sump lubrication system and four-speed transmission to the flathead model, refining it even more in the process. There was more to come: for 1940, the larger UH engine was given forged aluminum cylinder heads that had deeper fins for improved heat dissipation. The heads were lighter in weight as well, and brass sparkplug inserts were cast in to help prevent stripped threads during plug changes. UL customers could also order the silicon-aluminum heads as options, making them choice items for collectors today. While the flathead Big Twins remained popular into the 1940s, production ceased on virtually all civilian models when war broke out so that Harley-Davidson could focus its production on the smaller 45-cubic-inch WLA used by the U.S. armed forces throughout World War II. A limited number of UL models were produced during that time for specific civilian and military use, but for the most part the WLA constituted the bikes that Harley-Davidson built until the war ended in September 1945.

SPECIFICATIONS

Engine Displacement:	74 cubic inches
Transmission:	4-speed
Price:	$385

LORE

- Semicircular floorboards were equipped on Harley models starting in 1940.

- 3,893 ELs were built in 1940, compared to 822 ULs.

1942 MODEL WLA

Harley-Davidson did more than just paint its civilian-issue WL with olive drab paint, garnish the sheet metal with U.S. Army insignias, and slap a rifle scabbard on the fork before sending this bike into combat. No, the Motor Company devoted as much time and money to preparing this bike for combat as the U.S. Army spent on the recruits who would ride it into battle. Look closely at this war bike and you see special attention that made it field-ready. Gone are the WL's familiar art deco fenders, replaced with the more agrarian-styled raised mudguards developed to help prevent clogging under muddy conditions. There's also a sturdy rear fender rack to carry ammo and canteen supplies, and the saddlebags were cut to military specs so they could stow the important documents that couriers would transport from one post to the next. Special blackout lighting made the WLA harder to see under nighttime conditions, and the 18-inch tires' blocked tread pattern was better for off-road use than on pavement. Clearly, Harley-Davidson was out to help win the war with this model.

SPECIFICATIONS

Engine Displacement:	45 cubic inches
Weight:	576 pounds
Wheelbase:	57.5 inches
Number Produced:	13,051

LORE

- The WLA actually sold for 16 cents less than the civilian WL.
- All WLAs are labeled as 1942 models, regardless of year of manufacture.

1951 MODEL G SERVI-CAR

By 1951 the Model G Servi-Car had established itself as a mainstay in Harley-Davidson's lineup. Originally intended to help with roadside service of broken-down cars and for other quick-use jobs by small businesses, the three-wheeler eventually evolved into a workhorse for city governments and commercial agencies across the nation. The Servi-Car was ideal for police departments because the trike could remain unattended without being propped on a side stand while the police officer tended to the business of issuing a parking citation to any wayward motorist who overshot his or her meter time. And because the trike was easy to ride, police forces were able to hire women to ride them on the parking-meter beat. Of course the Servi-Car served in other ways, but its role in parking meter enforcement is probably what it will be most remembered for in years to come.

SPECIFICATIONS

Engine Displacement:	45 cubic inches
Wheelbase:	61 inches
Weight:	1,360 pounds

LORE
• The first Servi-Car appeared in 1932.
• The last Servi-Car was made in 1973.

CHAPTER TWO

SETTING THE WORLD STANDARD: THE KNUCKLEHEADS

Thirty-three years after manufacturing its first motorcycle, what became known as Serial No. 1, Harley-Davidson Motor Company rocked the establishment with their first overhead-valve Big Twin. The Model E, later to gain the affectionate nickname "Knucklehead," took the industry by storm.

Even though the overhead-valve engine concept was not new, the fact that Harley-Davidson was willing to produce it in mass quantities in 1936 was significant. Low-quality metallurgy and poor grades of gasoline at the time made it difficult to build an internal combustion engine that could sustain the kind of heat generated by high-compression cylinders. Moreover, America, like the rest of the world, was mired in an economic depression, so taking a financial risk on such a grand engineering project as the Model E could have proven disastrous.

And so, when Harley dealers from across the country gathered in the Green Room of Milwaukee's Schroeder Hotel for the first company dealers' meeting in five years, they did so with trepidation. It was with great hope that chief engineer William S. Harley, accompanied by the company's promotions man, "Hap" Jameson, unveiled the new bike, and it became clear that the American motorcycle industry was about to change forever.

1936 MODEL EL

The overhead-valve engine in Harley-Davidson's 1936 E and EL models was advanced for its time, but the new Harley motorcycle experienced many minor mechanical problems that year, resulting in ongoing improvements throughout 1936 and into 1937 such as fully enclosed rockers. Initial E and EL engines had partially exposed rockers that sprayed oil onto the rider's legs. Fortunately the new rocker covers and gaskets could be retrofitted to earlier engines, keeping everybody happy. There were, of course, many other improvements, such as revised head castings that addressed reliability and cooling issues, new oil fittings to minimize leakage, a larger and stronger clutch release finger, and more. And it all amounted to better overhead-valve engines with each passing year.

SPECIFICATIONS

Engine Displacement:	61 cubic inches
Weight:	565 pounds
Wheelbase:	59.5 inches
Number Produced:	1,829

LORE

- The EL didn't earn its Knucklehead moniker until after the Panhead bowed in 1948.

- Horsepower for the E was rated at 37; the EL produced 40.

HARLEY-DAVIDSON
61 OHV

Sensation of the Motorcycle World

Bill Cummings, winner of the 500-Mile Indianapolis Automobile Sweepstakes Classic in 1934, gives his unqualified kick out of owning and riding this white 61 OHV. It's the kind of a motorcycle champion like.

Minus fanfare and ballyhoo, a new motorcycle has come on the scene and has taken the world by storm. Wherever ridden and shown, wherever ridden and owned, the new 61 OHV Harley-Davidson has caused a sensation. Here is a NEW motorcycle incorporating ideas the seasoned rider gives his immediate and unqualified approval. As one owner writes, "It's my dream come true."

From everywhere come the most enthusiastic praises for this super motorcycle. Its wonderful handling qualities, its snappy response, its ability to stand up and "take it" make this 61 OHV the outstanding motorcycle of today and the motorcycle of tomorrow. See this great motorcycle at your dealer's and put it through its paces.

HARLEY-DAVIDSON MOTOR CO., Milwaukee, Wis., U.S.A.

1941 MODEL FL

Bigger is better, right? Not always, but there's no question that in 1941, when Harley-Davidson produced its first 74-cubic-inch overhead-valve engine, the Knucklehead line got better. Customers now had a choice of the proven 61-inch E/EL models or the new and more powerful 74-inch F/FL pair. Like the EL, the FL engine had slightly higher compression for more horsepower and torque, an important commodity then as it is today. And power was what Harley-Davidson was looking for, because law enforcement agencies had specifically requested more power from the EL to level the playing field against speeders on our nation's highways. Other than increased power, there wasn't much else to distinguish the new FL from the established EL. Even so, the larger engine helped Harley-Davidson embark on a new road that emphasized power and performance. FL and EL production slowed measurably when America entered World War II at the end of the year, but when peace returned in 1945 Harley-Davidson placed a strong emphasis on getting as many FL models to war-weary customers as possible. The EL remained in the lineup, but from 1941 on the FL outsold it, making the bigger engine the most popular model in the lineup. Truly, bigger was better in this case.

SPECIFICATIONS

Engine Displacement:	74 cubic inches
Horsepower:	48 horsepower at 5,000 rpm
Weight:	535 pounds
Number Produced:	2,452

LORE

- FL production slowed immensely from 1942 through 1945 due to World War II.
- Harley sold 2,280 EL models and 2,452 FL models in 1941.

1946 MODEL EL

One way to tell a properly restored 1946 Harley-Davidson is by the amount of chrome parts that it has—or better yet, *doesn't* have. With World War II still fresh in people's minds, materials and resources remained hard-to-find. Among those scarce items was chromium for plating motorcycle parts, so Harley-Davidson relied on paint to give their new motorcycles some shine. For instance, the Big Twin's valve tappet guides were painted silver to help give the same bright effect as chrome plating, and wheel rims were given a coat of black paint or a color matching the bike's tins as well. But none of that really mattered to customers who were eager to just have a brand new motorcycle. And by year's end 2,098 customers were treated to new EL Knuckleheads. The FL remained the biggest seller, though, with 3,986 on record as being built and sold. The war was over. It was time to ride!

SPECIFICATIONS

Engine Displacement:	61 cubic inches
Transmission:	4-speed
Wheelbase:	59.5 inches
Number Produced:	2,098

LORE

- The steering head angle on the 1946 EL was repositioned to 30 degrees for improved handling.
- The new steering head angle didn't work as well as the previous dimensions.

1947 MODEL EL

As Harley-Davidson ramped up for production of its 1947 motorcycles, the engineers were finalizing configuration for a replacement Big Twin for the following year. With a collective eye on the future, Harley-Davidson decided to give the tried-and-tested Knucklehead engine only a few changes and improvements for what was to be its final year. Chief among the changes was to fit the tappet assemblies with an updated roller with needle bearings that replaced the roller bushings used for the previous 10 years. They also incorporated a new ignition timer. Otherwise, the EL and FL engines for 1947 were much the same as those pressed into duty the previous year. Perhaps the big news, though, was the issue of chrome plating. As proclaimed in the September 1946 issue of the Harley-Davidson Motor Company's enthusiast magazine—fittingly called *The Enthusiast*—more chrome was on the way. Wrote the editors: "We are doing everything within our power to supply more chrome, and there is more of it on our 1947 Harley-Davidsons than there has been for a long time." Truly, order had finally been restored to the world—at least as far as Harley enthusiasts were concerned!

SPECIFICATIONS

Engine Displacement:	61 cubic inches
Transmission:	4-speed
Wheelbase:	59.5 inches
Number Produced:	4,117

LORE

- In 1947, for the first time, Harley-Davidson's catalog included the company's now iconic black leather jacket.

- To increase manufacturing capacity, Harley-Davidson purchased the Capitol Drive plant in Milwaukee in 1947.

1947 MODEL FL POLICE

Harley-Davidson offered either flathead or Knucklehead models to law enforcement agencies across the nation, but it was certainly the Knucklehead that was most favored by police officers themselves. And they preferred the FL model because the larger-displacement engine gave them the most performance. Police officers aboard Harley-Davidson police motorcycles reported for duty as early as 1909, when the city of Pittsburgh equipped its force with bikes from Milwaukee. Motor cops soon gained a reputation for nabbing speeders, and the *St. Louis Police Journal* even credited members of the city's motorcycle squad in a 1923 edition as doing "splendid work capturing speeders." Officers were also dispatched to crime scenes; early motorcycle radios had receivers only, so the officer couldn't acknowledge that he was on his way. He simply showed up! In addition to the dispatch radio, the motorcycles were equipped with emergency items, such as a first-aid kit, fire extinguisher, pursuit lights, and front fender "Police" placards. And for riding comfort, many officers didn't hesitate to pad their solo saddles with soft sheepskins!

SPECIFICATIONS

Engine Displacement:	74 cubic inches
Horsepower:	48 horsepower at 5,000 rpm
Wheelbase:	59.5 inches
Wheels:	16 inches front and rear

LORE
- Police radios by RCA were first installed on bikes in 1935.
- California Highway Patrol motor cops escorted military convoys along the coast during World War II.

CHAPTER THREE

BIG TWINS:
THE PANHEADS

When World War II ended in 1945, Americans were eager to resume their daily lives. Harley-Davidson was anxious to get on with their normal routine, too, and one matter of business was to update the overhead-valve Big Twin engine that was first released in 1936. The result was an engine with self-adjusting hydraulic lifters, aluminum cylinder heads, and a new set of rocker covers that resembled cooking pans. Within no time the engine was dubbed "Panhead" by Harley fans, who were eager to distinguish the new V-twin from the original OHV model. Fittingly, they applied the Knucklehead moniker to the original engine at about the same time, and both names have stuck ever since.

The first Panhead was probably released prematurely in 1948 and underwent a few needed improvements during the following years. Within a few years Harley enthusiasts also realized that there was no replacement for displacement, and soon enough the 61-cubic-inch E and EL models were dropped because demand favored the larger 74-cubic-inch F and FL versions of the Panhead.

Indeed, it was during the Panhead years that the company introduced the most technological improvements for the Big Twin. The hydraulic front fork was added to the FL in 1949 and, nine years later, rear suspension. By 1965, the last year for the Panhead, an electric starter motor was incorporated to the engine. Not until electronic fuel injection was incorporated into the lineup in the 1990s did the Big Twin—the Evolution (Evo) in this case—experience such radical improvements.

1949 MODEL FL

Harley's 1949 OHV twins checked in with a new name: the Hydra-Glide, referring to the hydraulically damped fork that replaced the age-old friction-damped springer. Big Twin engines were available in four states of tune and two displacements: the 61-cubic-inch engines E and EL (high compression), and the 74-cubic-inch F and FL (high compression). According to sales records, Harley-Davidson sold 3,419 ELs, compared to 8,014 FLs. And even though the new Big Twin model wore a designated name badge of Hydra-Glide, enthusiasts eventually pinned the unofficial label of Panhead to it because the engine's new stamped-steel rocker covers resembled cooking pans. Consequently, many of those same enthusiasts also adopted a nickname for the original E and F models, the Knucklehead.

SPECIFICATIONS

Engine Displacement:	74 cubic inches
Weight:	580 pounds
Wheelbase:	59.5 inches
Number Produced:	8,014

LORE
- The springer fork remained an option for 1949.
- The Model S, with its 125cc two-stroke engine, was the top seller in 1948, but the FL was tops for 1949.

1952 MODEL FL

A new foot shifter and hand clutch lever greeted customers for 1952. The familiar tank shifter with foot clutch mechanism remained, but to help spread its customer base Harley-Davidson equipped the Panhead models with the more conventional (by international standards) foot shift/hand clutch design. A few other lesser improvements were introduced for the model year, too, but for the most part the 1952 Panhead was a continuation of what had already been offered for a few years. Perhaps the big news from Milwaukee in 1952 was the introduction of K Model, a bike with a 45-cubic-inch flathead engine intended to compete head-on with the lightweight bikes from Europe. The K's engine had unit construction, too, and like the Panhead's new option, it had a foot shifter and hand clutch as standard equipment. Chrome-plated accessories continued to be the order of the day, with many of the optional shiny bolt-on parts available through the company's growing parts and accessories catalog.

SPECIFICATIONS

Engine Displacement:	74 cubic inches
Horsepower:	55 horsepower at 4,800 rpm
Weight:	590 pounds
Ignition:	6-volt

LORE

- 1952 was the first year for the new K Model, the predecessor to the Sportster, which bowed five years later.
- The 61-cubic-inch Panhead was dropped from the line after 1952.

1954 MODEL FLF POLICE BIKE

By 1954 the Indian Motorcycle Company was out of business, leaving Harley-Davidson as the lone supplier of police bikes, and the model of choice was the FL, one of the fastest production motorcycles of its time. The on-board radios were more sophisticated, allowing two-way transmitting so the officer could be in touch with other officers and the dispatcher at the police station. Safety and emergency equipment could be affixed to the bike for easy reach by the officer, and to help the engine from overheating in traffic, the FLE engine had milder camshaft lobes.

SPECIFICATIONS

Engine Displacement:	74 cubic inches
Transmission:	4-speed
Horsepower:	60 horsepower at 4,800 rpm
Wheelbase:	59.5 inches

LORE

- Police models had optional large-capacity oil tanks to help engine cooling in traffic.
- Gas masks were optional equipment, provided for the officer in the event of civil unrest.

1956 MODEL FL

Harley-Davidson's two leading models in terms of sales for 1956 remained the FLHF and the ST. The Big Twin engines received a few minor improvements for the year, such as a crankcase with internal galleys that delivered oil to the top end via a spring-operated oil-pump check valve. And a new 7-inch-diameter stainless steel air-cleaner cover gave the 1956 engine a distinctive look over earlier Panheads. The speedometer face received luminescent numerals that were easier to read and a brighter, red indicator needle.

SPECIFICATIONS

Engine Displacement:	74 cubic inches
Horsepower:	55 horsepower
Transmission:	4-speed
Number Produced:	856

LORE

• Foot-shift FLs continued to outsell the hand-shifters.

• Elvis Presley must have been impressed by the 1956 FL, because the following year he bought one.

1956 MODEL FLHF

By 1956, and with the demise of the Indian Motorcycle Company a couple years earlier, Harley-Davidson was essentially the only motorcycle company in America. That didn't mean there was no competition, because European and English brands were knocking loudly on the door, becoming more and more popular in this country. In fact, Norton racers had won the prestigious Daytona 200 from 1949 through 1952, and BSA-mounted Bobby Hill won in 1954. These victories brought notoriety to the lightweight English bikes that also had foot-shift transmissions. While Harley-Davidson equipped the new K Model's single-unit engine with a foot-shifter, they also adapted the FL's remote-mounted transmission with that feature, too. This particular FLHF sported an engine with higher compression than the FL, plus foot shifting that made it easier for new riders to adapt. The following year Harley-Davidson would inch even further away from an age-old standard—the 1957 model was the last of the FLs to use a rigid frame, and the 1958 FL ushered in a whole new era for the Milwaukee-born Big Twins.

SPECIFICATIONS

Engine Displacement:	74 cubic inches
Horsepower:	60 horsepower
Wheelbase:	59.5 inches
Number Produced:	2,315

LORE

• For the most part, the entire 1956 line reflected what was offered for 1955.

• America began building its interstate system in 1955.

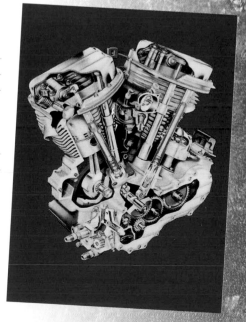

1960 MODEL FL

The 1958 FL checked in with a new name—the Duo-Glide, a moniker paying homage to the two hydraulically damped shock absorbers that provided suspension for the rear wheel. Although the upgraded rear suspension assembly added weight to the bike, it also improved its ride and handling. The redesign also allowed the engineers to develop a hydraulic rear brake for the FL. The new brake was easier to operate and more reliable than the older cable-linkage design found on the rigid-frame models. The new chassis established the Duo-Glide as a frontline motorcycle, and the improvements were so good that few changes were made to the model over the next two years. For the most part the changes simply enhanced the bike's cosmetics and selling appeal. A neutral indicator light was added to the gas tank instrument panel, new chrome trim could be found on the fenders, and the footboards were given a new finish for 1959. The following year the headlight nacelle was restyled, and the handlebar became *handlebars*—they were now a two-piece design that was centrally seated by a clamp. A few internal improvements to the engine offered more reliability and better oil control, and the rear shocks were recalibrated for a softer ride.

SPECIFICATIONS

Engine Displacement:	74 cubic inches
Weight:	670 pounds
Wheelbase:	60 inches
Top Speed:	100 mph

LORE

- By 1960 FL customers had a bevy of optional accessories with which to dress their bikes, leading to the name "dressers."
- Originally, the *H* in FLH meant that the engine had polished ports and more aggressive cam timing.

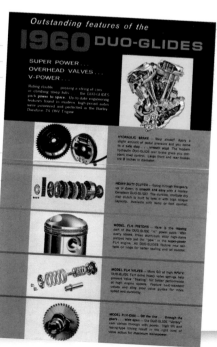

1963 MODEL FLH

By 1963 it was becoming apparent among industry insiders that few motorcycle enthusiasts in America favored the old tank-shifting method anymore. Indeed, using model sales as a barometer, records show that Harley-Davidson produced 2,100 FLHFs (foot-shift) compared to only 100 FLHs (tank-shift). Interestingly, the FLH outsold its FLHF stablemate 1,096 to 950, so the old guard was still making a statement, although fewer and fewer new-generation enthusiasts were listening. Regardless of which transmission shifting mechanism was most favored, Harley engineers continued making incremental improvements to the Panhead engine, and in 1961 the Big Twin's waste-spark ignition system was replaced with a superior dual-points/dual-fire ignition. And, as you might expect, minor cosmetic changes found their way onto all FL models each year, and in 1963 oil lines were routed externally for the first time since the Knucklehead era, when oil galleys were first used. But what warmed the hearts of many FL owners was the optional dual-exhaust system with chromed fishtail tips and the fiberglass saddlebags—integral components for many Harley-Davidson FL owners today. It seems that the more things change, the more they remain the same!

SPECIFICATIONS

Engine Displacement:	74 cubic inches
Transmission:	4-speed
Wheelbase:	60 inches
Price:	$1,425

LORE

- By 1963 Harley-Davidson marketed several small-displacement models.
- Harley's first scooter was the A Model, better known as the Topper, introduced in 1960.

1964 MODEL FL

While nearly 6,000 new FL customers still faced the ordeal of having to kick-start their big engines in 1964, Harley-Davidson engineers were secretively putting the finishing touches on a new electric starter motor for the venerable Panhead. The following year the 17-year-old engine design was updated with what soon became affectionately known as the "electric leg"—better known as the electric starter motor. With the push of a single button FL owners could sit back and enjoy as their engines fired to life. The time-honored ritual of kicking an engine through so that the proper cylinder was near top dead center for the kick-through, was a thing of the past. A flick of the thumb was all that was needed in 1965, and the new model would be called the Electra-Glide. In the meantime, customers who bought 1964 Duo-Glides had to rely on the kick pedal, a strong leg, and a little savvy to know just how to wake up that slumbering engine in the morning.

SPECIFICATIONS

Engine Displacement:	74 cubic inches
Horsepower:	54 horsepower at 5,400 rpm
Top Speed:	100 mph
Wheelbase:	60 inches

LORE

- Records show that an equal number of 1964 FL and FLH models were sold—2,725 each.
- By comparison, only 25 Topper scooters were produced that year.

CHAPTER FOUR

MINIMUM HOG:
THE SMALL HARLEY® MOTORCYCLES

Historically, American motorcycle enthusiasts have favored bikes with large-displacement engines. Bigger is better in their eyes, which helps explain why many of the popular models sold in America for the first half of the twentieth century were powered by engines displacing 45 cubic inches and more.

But America began to prosper after World War II more than it had in any other time in the nation's history. The influx of money meant more disposable income for Americans, and one thing that intrigued people in this country was the prospect of owning a motorcycle. A new term, "beginner bike," was coined, and by 1948 Harley-Davidson added the Model S to the lineup. The Model S was like

no other Harley before; it was powered by a single-cylinder 125cc two-stroke engine that barely produced five horsepower. But it was enough to entice more than 10,000 customers to buy it and try it.

Over the years the Model S's engine grew to displace 165cc and even 175cc. Various other models were included into the lineup as well, many of them using these larger small-bore engines. But by the late 1960s the writing was on the wall, and it read that Americans still preferred big bikes to little ones. By 1980 the smallest displacement engine to wear the Bar & Shield logo was the Sportster.

1948 MODEL S

At the close of World War II, Harley-Davidson obtained rights to copy and produce the DKW 125cc single-cylinder two-stroke engine as part of the war reparations from Germany. The compact engine, which was mated to a three-speed foot-shift transmission, developed 1.7 horsepower. In mid-1948 the company introduced its first motorcycle powered by this engine, the Model S. The new "peanut" tank carried 1.875 gallons of gas/oil pre-mix. It returned 70 miles to a gallon of fuel and could reach 35 to 40 miles per hour. This was a tremendously successful model for Harley-Davidson. The company manufactured 10,117 of these lightweights, a figure that accounted for one-third of all Motor Company production for 1948. This bike sold for $325.

SPECIFICATIONS

Price:	$325
Power Output:	1.7 horsepower
Top Speed:	40 miles per hour
Engine Type:	Two stroke single

LORE

- Harley-Davidson obtained the rights to copy the DKW 125cc single-cylinder two-stroke engine as part of war reparations from Germany.
- The Model S was Harley's first production two-stroke engine.

An advertisement for the 1960 Super 10.

1955 MODEL ST

In 1948 Harley introduced the Model S, a small, affordable bike powered by a 125cc two-stroke engine. The Model S originated as war reparations from Germany after World War II, when the Allied Forces were awarded blueprints of the DKW RT125. Birmingham Small Arms (BSA) of England was also awarded rights to build the small runabout. The tiddler engine produced about 2 horsepower and had a foot-shift three-speed transmission. The original Model S had a rigid frame with a girder-style fork that was updated to a Tele-Glide (telescopic type) in 1951. For 1953 engine displacement was stretched to 165cc, creating the Model ST, which remained in the lineup through 1959.

SPECIFICATIONS

Engine Displacement:	165cc
Transmission:	3-speed
Horsepower:	7 horsepower
Weight:	170 pounds

LORE

- Patent rights for the RT125 were also given to Japan, resulting in the first-ever Yamaha motorcycle in 1955.
- The peanut-shaped tank on the 1948 Model S inspired the name for the 2010 Forty-Eight.

1956 MODEL KH

The K Model was produced for only a few years—from 1952 through 1956—but it turned out to be a watershed period because the bike helped establish Harley-Davidson as a player in a changing market that included foreign brands. British and Italian bikes, especially, were gaining a foothold in the American marketplace, and the 400-pound K Model was just the answer to help stem the tide. The K boasted a unit-construction engine, making for a compact and lightweight motorcycle. The foot-shift lever was positioned on the right side of the engine—as was popular with the Brit bikes—and the K had rather strong brakes (for the time), so that it would whoa as well as it could go. To boost performance Harley-Davidson offered variations of the engine that led to the KH in 1954, and the following year the KHK, sporting hotter cams, found its way into the lineup. The KHK brought the fight to the invading British bikes, but Harley-Davidson had even more in store, and in 1957 the Sportster model was pressed into duty. The Sportster, or XL, engine shared the same basic bottom end with the K, but the overhead valves made it a far better source of power.

SPECIFICATIONS

Engine Displacement:	55 cubic inches (883cc)
Horsepower:	38 horsepower at 5,200 rpm
Weight:	400 pounds
Wheelbase:	56.5 inches

LORE

- Harley's race team used the flathead K engine for Class C competition until 1970.
- The race-prepped K engine displaced 750cc (45 cubic inches).

1963 MODEL BTH SCAT

The BTH Scat first appeared in the lineup for 1962, and the following year it received the new frame also found on the Pacer. The new frame had a rear swingarm system with a horizontal single spring that monitored the swingarm's movement beneath the engine—much like the design of the current-day Softail that first bowed in 1984. Now with full suspension front and rear, the BTH Scat offered acceptable handling for either off-road or on-road applications, which accounted for its rather Sportster-like design. For $495 a BTH Scat customer got a bike powered by a 175cc engine with upswept exhaust, 18-inch wheels and tires, a full suspension for big-bike handling, and high-clearance fenders that helped project a more off-road image. The solo seat was also sprung, making this dual-purpose motorcycle quite a bargain for its time. The BTH series evolved into the Bobcat, which lasted through the 1966 model year. But with the acquisition of Aermacchi in 1960 Harley-Davidson management turned to the Italian company to supply its lightweight models, and so the BTH—a model that began as the S in 1948—was quietly removed from production. This was the final small-bore model that Harley-Davidson built in America.

SPECIFICATIONS

Engine Displacement:	175cc
Engine Type:	2-stroke
Transmission:	3-speed
Number Produced:	877

LORE

- The BTH Scat's rear suspension was known as the Glide-Ride.

- The BTU had an intake restrictor that limited horsepower to five to comply with various insurance regulations of the time.

1965 TOPPER

The Topper is the only Harley-Davidson scooter ever to start with a rope-pull mechanism. The manual starter rope is located on the floor in front of the seat. Pulling the rope turns over a 9-horsepower, 165cc two-stroke single-cylinder. The rear body is fiberglass with a storage compartment under the seat. Harley-Davidson introduced the Model AH Topper in 1960 and kept them in production through 1965.

SPECIFICATIONS

Price:	$445
Power Output:	9 horsepower
Bodywork:	Fiberglass
Engine Type:	Two-stroke

LORE

- The Topper was capable of speeds up to 60 miles per hour.
- The Topper was introduced for the 1960 model year.

1995 MT500

Despite the MT500's fulfillment of its patriotic duty with the United States military, many Harley-Davidson historians and history books fail to mention it. That's too bad, because the MT500 proved especially useful for desert warfare in places like the Middle East, where rugged terrain requires a bike with ability to cope with all kinds of conditions. The MT500 was originally designed and built by Italy's SWM Motor Works, which was ultimately acquired by Armstrong Equipment of North Humberside, England. By 1987 Harley-Davidson had secured design and manufacturing rights for the Rotax-based bike, and assembly for the military model continued in York, Pennsylvania, until production ceased in 2000. By that time the MT500 had received electric starting, among other improvements. MT500-based variations were used by several militaries, including armed forces in Canada and Jordan, as well as the U.S. Armed Forces and those from Great Britain. But American race enthusiasts will recognize the MT500 engine as the single-cylinder motor that Harley-Davidson's race team used so successfully for its short-track bikes in the American Motorcyclist Association (AMA) Grand National Championship series.

SPECIFICATIONS

Engine Displacement:	30 cubic inches
Horsepower:	26 horsepower at 6,250 rpm
Weight:	370 pounds
Starter:	Electric and kick

LORE

- An MT350 (350cc) appeared in 1993.
- Several countries use the MT500 for military service.

CHAPTER FIVE

COMPETITION HOT:
THE SPORTSTER® MODELS

Harley-Davidson has been making Sportster motorcycles for more years than some motorcycle companies have been in business. That's a fact, and it's also a fact that the Sportster today remains a viable part of Harley-Davidson's new-model sales.

The first Sportster model, also known as the XL, was released in 1957 and represented little more than an update to the K Model. The biggest difference between the two models was the engine—the K relied on flathead combustion chambers, while the new Sportster had more modern overhead valves feeding hemispherical combustion chambers.

There was another difference, too: the Sportster models were certainly a heck of a lot faster than the old K Models. In California, where motorcycle racing was extremely popular, dealers were among the first to realize this and almost immediately asked the factory to produce a hotter set of camshafts for their customers' bikes. And so was born the XLCH. For the next 10 or so years the Sportster model had a reputation on the streets of America as one of the fastest and quickest motorcycles sold in this country.

1963 SPORTSTER® XLCH

Shortly after the Sportster model's debut in 1957, Harley engineers began to make the new bike faster, resulting in the XLCH. Harley-Davidson confidently claimed one horsepower per cubic inch from its 55-cubic-inch engine. *Cycle World* magazine called the potent Sportster model "clearly the fastest mass-produced motorcycle we have had." XLCHs had a reputation for starting on one kick; the question owners asked themselves every time they straddled the bike was: which one? And about that name, XLCH: certain California dealers had requested a hotter cam for the new model, and by 1958 Harley obliged. To this day, enthusiasts believe the myth that the CH stands for either California Hot or Competition Hot, but the actual meaning is not known.

SPECIFICATIONS

Engine Displacement:	55 cubic inches
Horsepower:	55 horsepower
Weight:	480 pounds
Wheelbase:	57 inches

LORE

- Among the early drag racers to find success with the XLCH was Carl Morrow.
- Cook Neilson, who would later be editor for *Cycle* magazine, rode an XLCH during his college days.

1972 SPORTSTER®

Change always seems to come in incremental stages at Harley-Davidson, and the birth of the XL-1000 series is no exception. The story begins in 1972 when the Sportster model's engine displacement was increased from 883cc to 1000cc thanks to a wider cylinder bore. The bigger cylinder jugs required a revamp of practically the entire engine, but there was even more in store for 1973 with the introduction of an updated frame. Gone was the familiar center post from which stemmed the Sportster's signature solo seat, and a stylish two-passenger seat that conformed to the flow of the frame's tubing was set in its place. Even though Harley stylists had tinkered with several two-up seat designs—among them the optional boat-tail seat of 1970 to 1971—it was the seat first used in 1972 that seemed to set the tempo for all future Sportsters. The frame also had its steering head angle pulled in one degree, from 30 to 29 degrees, and a new Kayaba fork from Japan (yes, Japan) helped counter the bumps in the road. By 1973 there was also a hydraulic disc brake posted up front, a first for any Harley-Davidson motorcycle.

SPECIFICATIONS

Engine Displacement:	61 cubic inches (1000cc)
Horsepower:	61 horsepower
Weight:	492 pounds
Quarter-mile:	13.38 seconds/97.70 mph

LORE

- Harley's 1973 lineup included the Shortster, a minibike powered by a 65cc engine.
- Within two years Sportster models would outsell the FLH by a ratio of two to one.

1977 XLCR SPORTSTER®

There's probably not a more iconic Sportster model than the XLCR; its styling was so different that many motorcycle enthusiasts in 1977 were caught off guard. After all, Harley-Davidson was a motorcycle company known more for its rawboned custom-style models than for elegantly streamlined café racers. Turns out that the general motorcycle community knew something that Harley-Davidson's marketing department didn't, because the black XLCR was a sales flop. Even so, it had a few redeeming values in terms of future models. The XLCR was the first Harley model to wear three disc brakes and cast aluminum wheels, and the bike's triangulated frame was perhaps the best yet for a Sportster. The XLCR lasted only two years in the lineup before it was dropped like a hot potato. And in 1978 Harley introduced a revamped XLH, a Sportster model that shared the same frame, aluminum wheels and triple-disc brake setup first found on the XLCR. The cruiser-based XLH also sold much better than the low-slung café racer. More than 11,000 XLHs were produced that year, compared to only 1,201 XLCRs, of which many remained on dealers' showroom floors for years to come.

SPECIFICATIONS

Engine Displacement:	61 cubic inches (1000cc)
Horsepower:	68 horsepower
Weight:	515 pounds
Wheelbase:	58.5 inches

LORE

• Willie G. Davidson designed the XLCR Café Racer.

• The XLCR's gas tank held four gallons—large for a Sportster model of the era.

1984 XR1000

Historians might question why the XR1000 was ever built. Some authorities suggest that Harley-Davidson felt that a high-performance model was needed in the lineup. Others are convinced that there had been a long-standing debate within the corporate structure that a model paying homage to the successful XR750 racer was essential to the brand's image. Regardless, the XR1000 first saw the light of day in the 1983 model year, and it created quite a stir, mainly due to an engine that was based on the XR750 racer, enabling the bike to carry a pair of Dell'Orto carburetors—just like the two-carb setup on the racer. Its upswept megaphone-style exhaust pipes on the left side were similar to those on the racer, too. But then there was the XR1000's frame and body ware, and to the untrained eye those components made this otherwise exciting and stellar motorcycle look like a humdrum Sportster model. Even so, the XR1000 and its $6,995 price tag served as a valuable marketing tool because it brought people into the showroom for a look. And most of the time those same curious customers rode out after they bought a new XLX priced at a modest $3,995. Curious what horsepower can do to somebody!

SPECIFICATIONS

Engine Displacement:	61 cubic inches
Horsepower:	70 horsepower
Weight:	490 pounds
Wheelbase:	60 inches

LORE

• *Cycle World* reported a quarter-mile time of 12.88 seconds for the XR1000.

• The XR1000 is perhaps the only mass-produced Harley model to have two carburetors.

2004 SPORTSTER® ROADSTER

When Harley-Davidson's director of marketing, Bill Davidson, introduced the 2004 Sportster line to the American motorcycle press, he described the totally revamped XL as blending "beautiful styling and exciting new technical features, yet [it] retains the character that has been the soul of the Sportster family since 1957." And in a nutshell, his analysis was spot on because while the 2004 Sportster models shared the same basic styling as earlier XLs, the new bikes were completely different in terms of technical features. Chief among the new improvements was the rubber-mounted engine, a concept that smoothed out the ride immensely. The new engine's mounting system required a stronger and much heavier frame, adding about 70 pounds to the package. Thicker frame tubes and heavier gussets marked the new frame, but it still didn't alter the bike's basic lines, so anybody not familiar with all the upgrades and changes for 2004 might mistake it for a slightly changed Sportster model. As the editors at *IronWorks* magazine wrote in their November 2003 issue: "The net effect, when coupled with the engine's refinements . . . translates to a much smoother-operating motorcycle."

SPECIFICATIONS

Engine Displacement:	74 cubic inches (1200cc)
Horsepower:	70 horsepower at 6,000 rpm
Weight:	557 pounds
Wheelbase:	60 inches

LORE

- An XL883 Roadster was also in the lineup, weighing 555 pounds.
- The XL883 engine produced 53 horsepower at 6,000 rpm.

2005 SPORTSTER® 883 CUSTOM

After the complete redesign of the Sportster model for 2004, subsequent years would see minor changes and refinements to the engine and rubber-mount frame. All models, the XL883 Custom included, received stylish headlights with a small Bar & Shield cloisonné affixed to the lens' center. Both Custom models—the XL1200C and the XL883C—differed from their Roadster counterparts, using forward foot controls, pull-back handlebars, sleeker and larger-capacity gas tanks, low-silhouette seats, and 21-inch front wheels to do so. The Customs were available in a variety of eye-catching colors, plus these boulevard cruisers checked in with more chrome than did the Roadsters.

SPECIFICATIONS

Engine Displacement:	883cc
Weight:	555 pounds
Wheelbase:	60 inches
Seat Height:	27.3 inches

LORE

- The XL883 Custom was one of four new models with the rubber-mounted engine.
- Pearl and two-tone paint jobs made the XL883 Custom a favorite among customers.

2006 XL883R SPORTSTER®

The XL883R sported a paint scheme and checkered graphics reminiscent of the factory XR750 flat-track racer. The sales literature of the time made the connection: "Check out the authentic H-D racing graphic and blacked-out parts. Twist the throttle and it's Saturday night at the racetrack." It wasn't particularly fast, but if looks could win races . . .

SPECIFICATIONS

Engine Displacement:	883cc
Weight:	560 pounds
Fuel Capacity:	3.3 gallons
Seat Height:	28.1 inches

LORE

- The 883R's graphics included checkered flags.
- Given the R's racy graphics, many enthusiasts felt it should have had the 1200cc engine.

2007 XL 883L
SPORTSTER® 883 LOW

Just as 2004 was a watershed year for the Sportster model, 2007 proved to be another landmark for the model: it marked the XL's 50th anniversary, making it the longest-running model ever for Harley-Davidson. To celebrate, Harley-Davidson updated the 883cc and 1200cc engines with electronic fuel injection (EFI). Carburetors were no longer used, and the EFI's more precise fuel metering not only reduced engine emissions, but also made them easier to start, smoothed out power delivery, and boosted performance. The smaller Sportster engine especially benefited from the new EFI, producing a claimed 18 percent gain in performance from 40 to 60 mph and a similar improvement during roll-on acceleration from 60 to 80 mph. But performance wasn't the only improvement. Fuel economy gained too, making the XL883 one of the most economical motorcycles of its class. And with a low seat height, the XL883L Low became one of the industry's sales leaders. By 2007, sales demographics pointed to more than four out of five first-time Harley-Davidson customers buying Sportster models, and more than a third of those owners were new to motorcycling.

SPECIFICATIONS

Engine Displacement:	883cc
Weight:	563 pounds
Seat Height:	26.3 inches
Fuel Economy:	45.0 mpg city/59.7 mpg highway

LORE

• The XL883L Low was joined by the XL1200L Low.

• Carburetion was no longer available on any Sportster model.

2008 XL1200N NIGHTSTER®

The XL1200N Nightster model represented a bold move by Harley-Davidson's marketing and styling teams because the new Sportster model deviated from the company's conservative tactics of evolving new designs slowly into the market. By chopping—or bobbing—the fenders, creating an all-new side-mounted license plate assembly, applying matte finish to the sheet metal, and blacking out much of the bike's trim, Harley stylists created a bike that looked like it rolled out of a back-alley chop shop rather than off the Motor Company's assembly line. Indeed, the tone of this model reeked with the bad-boy image that Harley-Davidson had for years tried to play down in public. Perhaps the writers at *Motorcyclist* magazine said it best, citing the Nightster model as being "better than brass knuckles in a bar brawl. Short of a used Sporty, a Sawzall, and a can of Krylon Hamm-R tone, you can't beat the Nightster for under $10K." But when all is said and done, the XL1200N is simply a variation of a time-honored model, the XL1200 Sportster. It's interesting what a little creative thinking can do to a Harley, isn't it?

SPECIFICATIONS

Engine Displacement:	74 cubic inches (1200cc)
Weight:	545 pounds
Seat Height:	26.3 inches
Wheel Sizes:	19 inches front, 16 inches rear

LORE

- In a nod to past Sportster models, the Nightster was given fork gaiters.
- Harley terms the finish to the Nightster model's engine cases "Rawboned."

2009 XL1200C SPORTSTER® 1200 CUSTOM

When you place your feet on the XL1200C Custom's forward-mounted foot controls, it's easy to forget that this is the smallest platform in the Harley-Davidson family of motorcycles. The Custom's ergonomics feel spacious to even the tallest of riders. For that reason, not to mention plenty of chrome-plated parts and colorful paint jobs, the Sportster Custom model is popular with men and women alike. By 2009 the Sportster Custom models—both the 883C and 1200C—enjoyed many improvements. The suspension's damping rates were recalibrated for a smoother ride, and the front fender was positioned closer to the tire for a more custom look. The aluminum slotted-disc rear wheel—by now a trademark for the XL Customs—was redesigned to shave four pounds from the previous design, in the process helping reduce unsprung weight for better handling and a softer ride. But it was the 1200 model that received slightly more chrome and such, so that everybody knew it was the alpha bike in the Sportster Custom family.

SPECIFICATIONS

Engine Displacement:	74 cubic inches (1200cc)
Weight:	562 pounds
Wheelbase:	60.4 inches
Wheels:	21 inches front, 16 inches rear

LORE

- The Sportster engine's four-cam arrangement allows for better valve angles in the cylinder heads.
- The first Sportster Custom model appeared in 1996, but it lacked forward foot controls.

NEW *LOOK*

NEW *POWER*

NEW *RIDING THRILL*

2010 SPORTSTER® XR1200

For a clear picture of what the XR1200 represents, you need only read what the editors at *Cycle World* magazine wrote about it in the August 2008 issue. In their words, the XR1200 was "without a doubt the best handling production Harley to date." It was a warrantable assumption, too, because from the beginning the XR1200 was developed to respond to rider input. To do that the XR1200's fork geometry was given precise measurements for snappy steering, its suspension's spring and damping rates were calibrated for quick response to road conditions, the brakes offer optimum stopping power, and to top off the package the Sportster engine was blessed with high-performance components, such as a 50 mm electronic fuel-injection throttle body and high-compression pistons. Mix this with body work and paint that takes many of its styling cues from the legendary XR750 racer and you have the best-performing Sportster model of all time. But that's not the end of the story. The second-generation XR1200X had even better suspension, making this a Harley motorcycle like no other before.

SPECIFICATIONS

Engine Displacement:	74 cubic inches (1200cc)
Weight:	562 pounds
Wheelbase:	59.8 inches
Seat Height:	29.2 inches

LORE

• The XR1200 formed the nucleus for the Vance & Hines XR1200 Road Race series.
• The XR1200 was originally intended only for the export market.

2011 FORTY-EIGHT® SPORTSTER®

Curiously, nowhere on the Forty-Eight Sportster model do you see the words "Forty-Eight." Nor does Harley-Davidson go out of its way to explain the name. It's just there. But what nobody has to explain to you about the Forty-Eight model is that this is a bike with attitude. Just listen to what some of the motorcycle press had to say: in the April 2010 report in *Thunder Press* we're told, "The Forty-Eight is Milwaukee's latest expression of their trademarked Dark Custom styling and attitude, and with the exception, in our view, of the Cross Bones, it's the most convincing effort to date." And in the June 2010 issue of *RoadBike*, ". . . the Forty-Eight straddles the tarmac like a steroid-fed, shoulder press-prone bully." Most of that attitude is attributed to the 16-inch balloon tires on painted spoke-laced rims, forward foot controls and a low handlebar, a low-profile seat that supports only the heartiest of riders, and the patented blacked-out paint scheme (with exception of the gas tank and a few chromed items). Now, about that name . . .

SPECIFICATIONS

Engine Displacement:	74 cubic inches (1200cc)
Weight:	567 pounds
Seat Height:	26.8 inches
Fuel Capacity:	2.1 gallons

LORE

- The Forty-Eight name pays homage to the 1948 Model S, the first time a Harley-Davidson model wore a peanut gas tank.
- The Model S was powered by a 125cc single-cylinder two-stroke engine.

2012 SPORTSTER® 1200 CUSTOM

For most people, the customized aspects of a stock Sportster 1200 Custom would be more than enough. With its in-your-face, fat-tired front end, brilliantly polished five-spoke cast wheels, new-for-2012 LED tail lamps, hand-finished fuel tank, and potent 1200cc fuel-injected V-twin Evolution engine, the stock bike is about as tricked-out a motorcycle as has ever rolled off of a factory assembly line. But some people just want a little bit more. For them, Harley offers the H-D1™ factory customization program exclusively for the 1200 Custom model. This program allows buyers to select from extended paint offerings, genuine H-D wheels, seats, handlebars, footpeg positions, and engine finishes.

SPECIFICATIONS

Length:	87.4 inches
Seat Height:	26.6 inches
Ground Clearance:	4.4 inches
Wheelbase:	59.9 inches

LORE

• The 1200 Custom has been in the Harley-Davidson lineup since 1996.

• The Sportster has been in production since 1957.

2013 SEVENTY-TWO

"Authentic '70s chopper attitude meets modern power and premium H-D styling in this bare-bones, lowrider-inspired radical custom," Harley-Davidson's marketing department proclaimed about the new XL1200V Seventy-Two. And rightly so—while the other Dark Customs hearkened back to the 1940s and 1950s, the Seventy-Two took its inspiration from the glitter and glam of the 1970s. While the Seventy-Two is available in non-gloss Black Denim and Big Blue Pearl paint, anyone who appreciates the '70s style of this machine will pony up for the period-correct Hard Candy Lucky Green Flake paint.

SPECIFICATIONS

Price:	$10,699–$11,424
Length:	89.4 inches
Rake:	30.1 degrees
Trail:	5.3 inches

LORE

- The Seventy-Two wasn't named for the size of its engine, but rather the year in which the bike's chopper-like styling and optional metal-flake paint was originally at its peak popularity.

- If you have a metal flake helmet to match the Seventy-Two's optional metal flake paint, you will be worshipped as a hipster god.

CHAPTER SIX

KINGS OF THE HIGHWAY:
THE TOURING BIKES

The term "King of the Highway" dates back to the days of the Panhead, when it described an optional touring accessory package for the FL model. The King of the Highway parts group included the Buddy Seat, saddlebags, and a multitude of chromed accessories. Eventually the term "dresser" worked its way into Harley lexicon, and that's what touring bikes were called for many years.

While the term "dresser" has taken a back seat to "touring bike" or "bagger," and the King of the Highway package group is no longer offered, there's no disputing that those dressed-up Panheads and Shovelheads were spectacular bikes to be seen on the highways of America.

Owners of Harley touring models today don't have to worry about adding the King of the Highway accessory group to their bikes because FLs today are distinguishable right off the showroom floor. Ever since the first Evolution-powered FL rolled into the light of day, the Motor Company has made sure that all of its touring models have the proper amenities and accessories to give their owners all-day comfort on long trips. The King is dead. Long live the King.

1966 ELECTRA-GLIDE®

The 1966 FLH Electra-Glide broke new ground for Harley-Davidson's flagship model. The engine's cylinder heads were patterned after those of the Sportster model, creating more efficient combustion chambers and resulting in a gain of about five horsepower for the FLH. The new cast-aluminum rocker boxes were noticeably different in shape from the Panhead's, leading enthusiasts to adopt the name "Shovelhead" for the new model. The optional King of the Highway accessory package included front and rear bumpers, Extra Quiet dual mufflers, Buddy Seat, crash bars, saddlebags, and a windscreen. The top-of-the-line FLH sold for $1,610.

SPECIFICATIONS

Engine Displacement:	74 cubic inches
Weight:	783 pounds
Fuel Capacity:	5 gallons
Horsepower:	60 horsepower at 5,400 rpm

LORE

- The FLH was the top-selling model for 1966.
- Big Twins were given 12-volt charging system in 1965 to power the new electric starter motors.

1966 NEVADA HIGHWAY PATROL

After the demise of the Indian Motorcycle Company in 1953, Harley-Davidson enjoyed a virtual monopoly as the primary supplier of motorcycles and trikes for the various police and civil service departments across the country. Consequently, many public agencies used either the Servi-Car trike or the FLH bike for patrol duty. For the most part, the Servi-Car was better suited to traffic control or monitoring parking violations. But when it came to chasing speeders on the highway, the best Harley model for the job was the FLH police edition. By the mid 1960s Harley-Davidson offered various equipment packages tailored to law enforcement agencies. Most packages included pursuit lights, sirens, fire extinguishers, two-way radios, and saddlebags or side boxes to carry miscellaneous items. Sirens were often powered by a generating system that made contact with either the front or rear tire. The officer would depress a lever with the heel of his boot so that the siren pivoted on its mount and the shaft made contact with the tire. Harley-Davidson also worked with the individual law enforcement agencies to determine what colors their bikes were to be painted and placement of the department's graphics and logo.

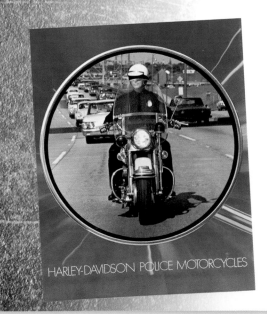

HARLEY-DAVIDSON POLICE MOTORCYCLES

SPECIFICATIONS

Engine Displacement:	74 cubic inches
Horsepower:	60 horsepower at 5,400 rpm
Wheelbase:	60 inches
Charging System:	12-volt

LORE

- Harley-Davidson experimented with a Sportster police model in the early 1960s.
- Police departments determined their own paint schemes for the officers' motorcycles.

1967 FLH ELECTRA-GLIDE®

Two consecutive years of major changes—electric starting in 1965 and a new top-end design in 1966 that resulted in the Shovelhead engine—was plenty for Harley-Davidson. And so, for 1967, engineering focused on refining the existing product line rather than making any more major changes. In the case of the FL and FLH, most of those refinements were confined to the chassis and body parts. The Electra-Glide model's fender tips were slightly reshaped for a bolder look, and turnout mufflers were added to the option list. The rear drum brake, axle, and spacers were modified for improved handling and braking performance, and front and rear wheel hubs were given sealed ball-bearings for more reliability and less upkeep. In terms of production numbers, Harley-Davidson sold slightly fewer Electra-Glide motorcycles in 1967 than it did in 1966, although the approximate ratio of two FLHs to one FL remained.

SPECIFICATIONS

Engine Displacement:	74 cubic inches
Oil Capacity:	4 quarts
Weight:	783 pounds
Wheelbase:	60 inches

LORE

- The leaky Linkert carburetor was replaced with the troublesome Tillotson.
- Harley-Davidson sold more than twice as many FLH models as FLs.

1967 FLH ELECTRA-GLIDE®
POLICE MODEL

No doubt, the addition of electric starters on Harley-Davidson motorcycles in 1965 made the big American-made bikes even more popular with law enforcement agencies across the nation. Thumb-starting an engine was much easier than having to kick-start it with your leg, an important concession for police officers who had to constantly mount and dismount their motorcycles in the course of their work shifts. And among those motorcycles favored by police officers was this 1967 FLH Electra-Glide Police Model, which came with its own special equipment. Contrast the squared metal saddlebags to the fiberglass saddlebags of the civilian Harley models. The cop bikes lacked much of the chrome trim of their civilian counterparts, too, but both editions shared similar powertrains based on their 74-cubic-inch engines, which were among the largest displacement motorcycle motors of their time.

SPECIFICATIONS

Engine Displacement:	74 cubic inches
Transmission:	4-speed
Fuel Capacity:	5 gallons
Wheelbase:	60 inches

LORE
- The California Highway Patrol established its motorcycle training program in 1960.
- The first Harley-Davidson police motorcycle was delivered to the Detroit Police Department in 1908.

1968 MODEL FLHFB
ELECTRA-GLIDE®

By 1968 the Electra-Glide model was gliding along as one of the Motor Company's more popular models. Electra-Glide owners and their passengers could be seen perched on their bikes' Buddy Seats while they cruised the highways and byways of America. Meanwhile, Harley-Davidson's advertising department concentrated on a marketing campaign to counter Honda's "You Meet the Nicest People" slogan with advertisements showing Harley owners in everyday situations with their bikes. One 1968 magazine ad for the Electra-Glide model read: "Introduce yourself to a one-of-a-kind experience. Ride the new Electra Glide. In this one motorcycle, you'll get the precise engineering of a formula racer and the handcrafted luxury of a custom roadster. Here too, are the stamina, balance and ride that have made the 1200 Electra Glide the world's foremost cycle. Now add electric starting, new instrumentation and futuristic styling. This is Electra Glide for 1968. On display now at the Harley-Davidson dealer nearest you. A limited edition of unlimited excellence. Stop in for a test ride soon." By year's end Harley-Davidson had produced nearly 7,000 Electra-Glide motorcycles—an impressive number for the time.

SPECIFICATIONS

Engine Displacement:	74 cubic inches
Weight:	7783 pounds
Wheelbase:	60 inches
Top Speed:	100 miles per hour

LORE

- Harley-Davidson's race team won 18 of 23 AMA Grand National races in 1968.
- Cal Rayborn lapped the entire field while winning the 1968 Daytona 200 aboard his KR750.

1969 ELECTRA GLIDE

Harley-Davidson owned the heavyweight touring bike market when it built this FLHFB Electra Glide. Powered by a 74-cubic-inch, overhead-valve Shovelhead engine coupled to a four-speed transmission, the Electra Glide represented the pinnacle of touring-bike technology at the time. "The Electra Glide's suspension provides the smoothest ride in the industry," factory literature proclaimed, "and the dual saddle is a classic of touring comfort."

SPECIFICATIONS

Engine Displacement:	74 cubic inches
Engine Type:	Overhead valve V-twin
Front Brake:	Drum
Rear Brake:	Drum

LORE

- The year 1969 marked the replacement of the generator-type bottom end with the alternator-type bottom end.

- The batwing fairing became available as a factory option for the first time in 1969.

1977 FLH ELECTRA-GLIDE®

The Electra-Glide model had undergone a few noticeable changes and improvements during the previous 10 years. Perhaps most notable was in 1969, when the front brake mechanism was relocated to the right side, and the following year, when the generator was replaced with a more superior alternator, requiring a new, conical right-side cover on the engine. By 1972 a front disc brake was anchored to the FL's massive fork, and the 1973 model featured single disc brakes front *and* rear. Gone was the kick-start pedal, plus the hand-shifter was eliminated in 1973, too. Made-in-America loyalists cringed in 1974 when a Japanese-made Keihin carburetor replaced the Bendix, and a year later the throttle cable was fitted with dual return springs. With only a few internal improvements for 1977, Harley-Davidson placed the FLH on the market wearing such touring refinements as hard saddlebags and a bat-wing fairing, not to mention grab rails and a backrest for the passenger. Little did people know at the time, but with this design Harley-Davidson was setting the touring standard for the coming years.

SPECIFICATIONS

Engine Displacement:	74 cubic inches
Weight:	760 pounds
Wheels:	16 inches front and rear
Brakes:	Single disc front and rear

LORE

• The last motorcycle Elvis Presley ever bought was a 1977 FLH Electra-Glide.

• Harley-Davidson's factory rider Jay Springsteen won the second of his three AMA Grand National titles in 1977.

1980 FLH ELECTRA-GLIDE®

Just look at a 1980 FLH, and it's apparent that Harley-Davidson was gaining a better appreciation for what touring enthusiasts liked: comfortable amenities on their bikes. They also liked those same bikes to shovel out power in giant scoopfuls, and that's precisely what FLH customers got when the new decade began. A locking Tour-Pak and saddlebags meant that riders not only could take it with them, but they'd keep it with them as well. Those locks kept a rider's gear safe and secure. Any question about power was silenced the moment the 80-cubic-inch Shovelhead engine fired to life. The larger engine offered more power than the standard-issue 74-cubic-inch mill. Indeed, the editors at *Cycle* magazine recognized Harley's biggest engine for what it was when they wrote in the November 1980 issue: "Eighty cubic inches strung out fore-to-aft would make any engine dominate the visual part of the whole; Harley-Davidsons have no trouble keeping the first part in motor cycle preeminent even though the bike is eight feet long."

SPECIFICATIONS

Engine Displacement:	80 cubic inches
Horsepower:	67 horsepower at 6,000 rpm
Transmission:	4-speed
Weight:	760 pounds

LORE

- The 74-inch engine was standard on FL models; the 80-inch engine was optional.
- The FLT debuted in 1980.

2003 ULTRA CLASSIC®
ELECTRA-GLIDE®

A year before Harley-Davidson celebrated its 100th anniversary for 2003, the touring models received larger swingarms and rear axles, new suspension calibrations, and an engine mounting system that was 250 percent stiffer than before, paving the way for some spectacular landmark styling treatments for their 100th Anniversary Edition models that would bow for 2003. Among the unique features were paint colors that would be offered one year only, so that Anniversary Edition models would forever stand apart from all other model years, as well as special cloisonné tank badges. No doubt the folks in Milwaukee were preparing to roll for another 100 years.

SPECIFICATIONS

Engine Displacement:	88 cubic inches
Weight:	788 pounds
Wheelbase:	63.5 inches
Fuel Capacity:	5 gallons

LORE

- Paint on virtually all 2003 Anniversary Edition Harley models was specific to that year.
- All 2003 models had Anniversary logos embossed on the seats and medallions on the engine crankcase.

2005 ROAD KING® CUSTOM

Not all custom Harley models are the product of artistic pro builders. Take, for instance, the Road King Custom. By performing a few tweaks here and there, Harley's stylists were able to present a Road King model different from all others. For starters, seat height is noticeably closer to the ground as well. You won't find as many identification badges and logos on the Custom either, and many of the components, such as floorboards and saddlebags, have their own new touches to further distance this model from the others. Yet the heart of the Road King Custom model remains the same as its siblings, meaning that it's powered by the Twin Cam 88 engine that was available with either a Keihin carburetor or electronic fuel injection in 2005. And like all Harley-Davidson motorcycles, customers could give their Road King Custom motorcycle a few additional components simply by shopping through the Genuine Motor Parts & Accessories catalog.

SPECIFICATIONS

Engine Displacement:	88 cubic inches
Transmission:	5-speed
Weight:	721 pounds
Seat Height:	28.3 inches

LORE

- The Road King Custom model sits about half an inch lower than the Standard.
- The Custom weighs two pounds less than the Standard.

2005 ROAD GLIDE®

Only one Road Glide model was available for 2005, and it checked in with features that might be considered options on other models. Electronic fuel injection was standard, as was a sound system that included a 40-watt-per-channel AM/FM/WB/CD player. Customers didn't have to check the box for cruise control either; it was included in the mix, along with silver powder coating on the engine, wheels, and calipers to further set the Road Glide model apart from other bikes. The signature frame-mounted fairing and its silver gauges remained part of the package too, and it wore silver graphics that continued onto the gas tank and saddlebags. Indeed, the aerodynamic fairing is the Road Glide model's signature trait, and it not only looks streamlined, it also offers better wind penetration than any other in Harley-Davidson's line. Road Glide riders have been known to get up to 10 percent better fuel economy than that delivered by the Electra-Glide model's bat-wing fairing.

SPECIFICATIONS

Engine Displacement:	88 cubic inches
Induction:	Electronic fuel injection
Weight:	731 pounds
Seat Height:	26.9 inches

LORE

- The FLTRI Road Glide and FLHTCUI Ultra Classic Electra-Glide were the only two models equipped with EFI standard.
- The FLT first appeared in 1980.

2006 FLHXI STREET GLIDE®

Lower, smoother, and stripped of chrome. That pretty much describes the FLHXI Street Glide, and when this minimalist touring, or dresser, model debuted in 2006 it rocked the establishment. Dressers were supposed to be staunch in design and concept. They were bikes ridden by older, more conservative riders. Or so some people thought, but when Harley-Davidson rolled the Street Glide model into the light of day, those perceptions flew right out the window. Look closely at the Street Glide motorcycle and you'll notice an absence of chrome trim that is generally associated with these big Harley models. But there's more—or actually less—to the FLHX, because it prompted Harley designers to reconfigure the contours of the saddlebags to improve not only looks, but handling as well, thanks to a lower center of gravity. The Street Glide model has many of its own styling touches as well, notably the floorboards and foot controls, a chromed and stretched fuel tank console with diamond-cut nameplate, and an abbreviated smoke-tint windscreen to maintain its low silhouette. Most of all, the Street Glide model made it acceptable for younger riders to be seen on a Harley-Davidson motorcycle with saddlebags and a wind fairing.

SPECIFICATIONS

Engine Displacement:	88 cubic inches
Transmission:	5-speed
Weight:	745 pounds
Seat Height:	26.3 inches

LORE

- The Street Glide model made it fashionable to be seen on a bagger.
- Harley-Davidson's marketing team described the FLHX as an "undressed dresser."

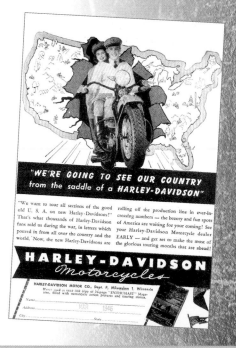

2007 FLHR ROAD KING®
FIREFIGHTER
SPECIAL EDITION

The events of September 11, 2001, have had profound repercussions on Americans, but rising from the ashes is this Firefighter Special Edition, first available in 2002. Given the exclusivity of this model, only a limited number were offered, and they were sold only to qualified buyers. Those buyers were—and remain—American firefighters. Once the buyer shows proof that he or she is a certified firefighter with a designated firefighting department within the United States, the order is processed and the motorcycle delivered to the nearest dealer. The owners are also given a special identification tag that can be attached to the bike. As you might guess, every Firefighter Special Edition is finished in fire-engine-red paint.

SPECIFICATIONS

Engine Displacement:	96 cubic inches
Weight:	740 pounds
Wheelbase:	63.5 inches
Seat Height:	29.9 inches

LORE

- The Firefighter Special Edition has special medallions, too.
- Scale-model replicas are also available from the Franklin Mint.

2007 FLTR ROAD GLIDE®

Harley-Davidson's big news for 2007 was the 96-cubic-inch engine. Based on the Twin Cam 88, the TC96 had a bundle of mechanical improvements. With the engine came a new transmission, the six-speed Cruise Drive. Carburetion was no longer standard, nor was it an option, so gone was the *I* that designated fuel-injected models. The FLTR Road Glide maintained its status as a single-type model as opposed to the multiple models enjoyed by the rest of the Touring family; there were three Road King models and Electra-Glide models, although it can be argued that while the Street Glide model is based on an Electra-Glide model, it is considered its own model. But to ensure that not every Road Glide motorcycle looked the same, Harley-Davidson offered nine color choices for paint.

SPECIFICATIONS

Engine Displacement:	96 cubic inches
Transmission:	6-speed
Weight:	761 pounds
Seat Height:	26.9 inches

LORE

• The silver powder-coated engine cases are a signature design feature on the FLTR.

• The 96-inch engine's air cleaner cover is more oval-shaped than the TC88's.

2009 FLHX STREET GLIDE®

For the 2009 model year Harley-Davidson completely revamped the chassis for the FLH and FLT models, giving the line a new frame and new spring and damping rates in the fork and shocks. Improvements to the engine mounting system helped stabilize the Big Twin engine, a stouter swingarm further steadied the bike's handling through corners, and the new frame was 20 percent stiffer than its predecessor. The rear wheel was wrapped with a new dual-compound tire that utilized a larger tread pattern, and subtle styling changes helped differentiate bikes like the 2009 Harley-Davidson FLHX Street Glide from previous models. To help minimize heat transmitted to the rider the exhaust header pipe was slightly rerouted so that it no longer looped behind the transmission.

SPECIFICATIONS

Engine Displacement:	96 cubic inches
Weight:	773 pounds
Wheelbase:	63.5 inches
Seat Height:	26.3 inches

LORE

- *Motorcyclist* magazine stated about the FL's handling, "The new touring bikes ride tighter from nose to tail."
- The new rear tire measured 180 mm across.

2010 ROAD GLIDE® CUSTOM

If they liked it once, they'll love it a second time. So thought Harley-Davidson's stylists, who recognized the sales success enjoyed by the Street Glide model could easily repeat itself with a similar version of the Road Glide model. And so was born the Road Glide Custom, a touring model boasting less chrome and more spunk. Foremost, the Custom presents a low profile, giving it a sleeker, more, well, *custom* look. Gone is the Tour-Pak luggage carrier and fluffy passenger seat, and the frame-mounted fairing is topped with the abbreviated smoke-tint windscreen favored by riders concerned with a bike's looks. Up front rolls a sporty 18-inch wheel wrapped with a lower profile 130/80x18 Dunlop tire. Even the floorboards are more stylish than those found on the standard-edition Road Glide model, and you won't see an obtrusive taillight and license plate assembly on the rear fender, either; in its place is a flush-fit LED taillight with a compact license plate mount.

SPECIFICATIONS

Engine Displacement:	96 cubic inches
Weight:	769 pounds
Seat Height:	25.8 inches
Fuel Capacity:	6 gallons

LORE

- The Road Glide Custom model sports a 2-into-1 collector exhaust.
- A 40-watt amplifier powers the audio system.

Smoothness and handling. This is what it's all about.

2010 STREET GLIDE® TRIKE

Among the first questions somebody asks when they see Harley-Davidson's Trike is, "How does it handle?" For that we'll defer to the August 2009 issue of *RoadBike* magazine, where the editors wrote: "The specific-to-this-model frame, with its increased fork angle and lessened trail, provides better steering than most trikes. The front forks are longer than those on two-wheeled Ultras and have an external steering stabilizer. The front wheel is a 16" hoop, the rears are 15-inchers." The Street Glide Trike was the second model of Harley-Davidson's second-generation three-wheelers (the first generation was the Servi-Car), and it takes many of its styling cues from its two-wheel cousin, the Street Glide model. Which, as you might guess, also explains why the two models share similar names. And like the Street Glide motorcycle, the Trike doesn't have the usual chrome trim and Tour-Pak luggage carrier, making it lighter than the Tri Glide Ultra Classic three-wheeler; the Tri Glide trike weighs 1,139 pounds compared to the Street Glide Trike's 1,070 pounds.

SPECIFICATIONS

Engine Displacement:	103 cubic inches
Transmission:	6-speed, optional electric reverse
Weight:	1,071 pounds
Wheelbase:	66.6 inches

LORE

- The Trike's trunk provides 4.3 cubic feet of storage space.
- Harley-Davidson offered the Servi-Car three-wheeler from 1932 through 1973.

2011 ROAD KING®

There's as much refinement and dignity in the Road King model's looks as there is in its name. With styling that's based ever so much on the Duo-Glide of the late 1950s and early 1960s, the Road King model commands attention from anyone who recognizes the classic lines of big-bore Harley motorcycles from that era. But when it comes to performance, ride and handling, those Duo-Glides must bow down to today's Road King model, because it boasts technical features that enthusiasts could only dream of 50 years ago. Three disc brakes, electronic fuel injection feeding a two-camshaft engine with an electric starter, a six-speed transmission, and a chassis that's taut through the turns and cushy-smooth over the bumps put their royal stamp on today's Road King model. Long live the King!

SPECIFICATIONS

Engine Displacement:	96 cubic inches
Weight:	775 pounds
Wheelbase:	63.5 inches
Seat Height:	26.5 inches

LORE

• The Road King model was introduced to the market in 1994.
• The first Road King motorcycle weighed 692 pounds.

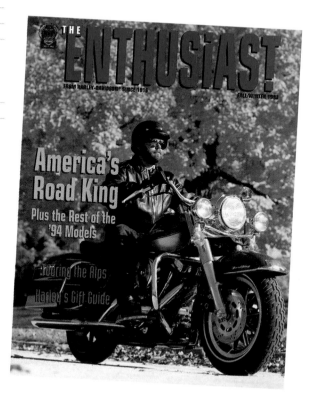

2012 SWITCHBACK

With the 2012 Switchback, Harley-Davidson brought together the best elements of two of its most popular product lines—the Dyna and the Touring motorcycles. Seemingly a union of opposites—the Dyna models represent the ultimate in cruisers and the Touring models represent the state of the art in luxury motorcycles—the end result brings vintage Harley-Davidson simplicity to motorcycle touring. With its detachable windshield and saddlebags, it's like having two bikes in one: a powerful, head-turning street cruiser that can also go the distance as a comfortable, easy-handling tourer.

SPECIFICATIONS

Rake:	29.9 degrees
Trail:	5.8 inches
Wheelbase:	62.8 inches
Weight:	696 pounds

LORE

- The Switchback captured the stripped-down styling of the original Harley-Davidson touring bikes.
- The Switchback was the first dedicated touring bike based on the Dyna chassis.

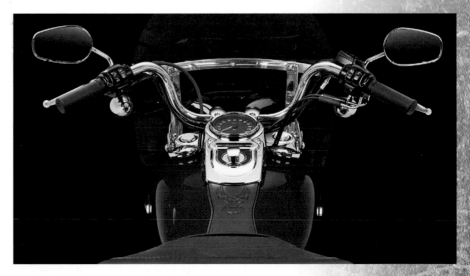

2012 ELECTRA GLIDE®
ULTRA LIMITED

When Harley-Davidson's design team set out to create the unmistakable style of the Harley-Davidson® Electra Glide® Ultra Limited motorcycle, part of their goal was to leave plenty of room for showing off the bike's lustrous paint. This had advantages beyond just resulting in a beautiful machine. The six-gallon fuel tank, for example, doesn't just create a bigger canvas for displaying custom paint; it holds six gallons, allowing owners to ride farther between pit stops. But let's not discount that stunning dual-color paint scheme, with its crisp pinstripes that run the length of the bike and special Harley-Davidson® tank medallions.

SPECIFICATIONS

Length:	98.6 inches
Wheelbase:	63.5 inches
Weight:	882 pounds
Luggage Capacity:	4.52 cubic feet

LORE

- The Electra Glide Ultra Classic Limited was the most well-appointed non-CVO model in Harley-Davidson's lineup.
- The Electra Glide is much more agile than its statistics would indicate because of a clever arrangement of its steering head.

CHAPTER SEVEN

FACTORY CUSTOMS:
LOW RIDER® AND WIDE GLIDE® MODELS

Nobody really planned on developing a factory custom. The concept just evolved, and in no time the motorcycle world would never be the same again.

Blame it on Willie G. Davidson, if you must. He's the one who designed the 1971 FX Super Glide model, considered the model that set the tone for things to come. Within a few years Willie and the boys tinkered some more with the Super Glide model, and wouldn't you know it, a whole new genre of Harley motorcycles was born.

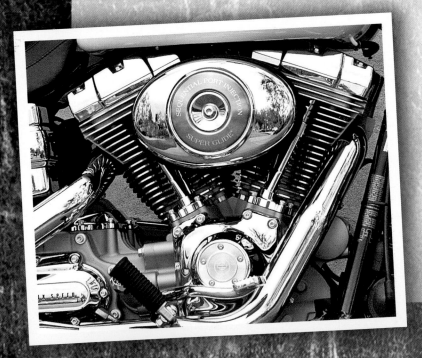

Factory-custom DNA can be traced back to the 1977 Low Rider model, revealing the first signs of the evolutionary process that continues to this day. Within three years the Wide Glide and Sturgis models followed, and eventually Harley-Davidson had momentum to produce some of the best factory-built customs the motorcycle world had seen yet. More customs were to follow, but those three models form the figurehead—the Mount Rushmore, if you will—of the factory custom world. And we owe it all to one creative mind with the gumption to place a Sportster front end onto a stripped-down FL.

Super Glide FX.
Call it the night train.

New 1200cc Super Glide FX. Ultimate superbike. The action-eager muscle machine that says move out! 74-inch engine for blinding performance. Big-inch power with Sportster-like styling. Stripped, long-travel fork. Trouble-free Bendix carburetor, high-output alternator. And cast, polished covers. One look tells you you're the man for this hot new muscle machine. Super Glide FX. The night train. From Harley-Davidson. Number one where it counts . . . on the road and in the records. AMF | HARLEY-DAVIDSON, Milwaukee, Wisconsin 53201.

1 the Harley-Davidson **outperformers**

1971 MODEL FX
SUPER GLIDE®

The motorcycle market experienced dramatic changes in the late 1960s and early 1970s as the Baby Boom generation came of age and began buying vast numbers of motorcycles, and these new buyers demanded a new style of motorcycle. To meet that demand, Chief Designer Willie G. Davidson created the 1971 FX Super Glide. This example is painted in what the Motor Company calls "Sparkling America"—white, with red, blue, and white Mylar panels on the fenders and tanks. The factory assembled 4,700 FX models in 1971, and this version sold for $2,230.

SPECIFICATIONS

Engine Displacement:	74 cubic inches
Price:	$2,230
Production:	4,700 units
Chief Designer:	Willie G. Davidson

LORE

- The original Super Glide was only available with a kick starter.
- Harley-Davidson officially mentioned the name "Night Train" in its period advertising.

**All new for 1971:
Super Glide**

Shown here in optional
"Sparkling America" paint style

1977 FX LOW RIDER®

The brewmeister for the 1977 Low Rider model was none other than Willie G. Davidson. The new Low Rider model looked long and lean, thanks in large part to its low 26-inch two-up saddle (hence the "Low" designation) and stretched-out 32-degree steering head angle (lending to the "Rider" portion of the name). When Willie G. and the boys deemed the Low Rider model fit to sell, Harley-Davidson dealers across the country tapped into the factory for their allotted shares of bikes to put on their showroom floors. And for good reason, because the Low Rider model outsold all other Harley models in 1977. Many enthusiasts today consider the 1977 FX Low Rider model as the first true factory-built custom motorcycle.

SPECIFICATIONS

Engine Displacement:	74 cubic inches
Transmission:	4-speed
Weight:	584 pounds
Fuel Capacity:	5 gallons
Seat Height:	26 inches

LORE

- The 1977 Low Rider and XLCR models were the first Harley motorcycles with dual-disc brakes.
- The FX's kick-starter was eliminated in 1979.

1980 MODEL FXWG-80 WIDE GLIDE®

One of the biggest corporate blunders in American history silently unfolded in 1980, when the movers and shakers at American Machine & Foundry—owners of the Harley-Davidson Motorcycle Company at the time—failed to recognize the significance of two new models, the FXB Sturgis, which featured belt drive, and the FXWG Wide Glide, which looked as much like a radical chopper as any production motorcycle ever has. No doubt, the Wide Glide model had it all—forward foot controls, a bobbed rear fender in contrast to the slim fender up front, staggered exhausts, a 41mm wide-glide fork from which the bike drew its name, a king-and-queen-style seat, and the most radical flamed paint job to ever find its way onto a motorcycle dealer's showroom floor. The avant-garde model was born on Willie G. Davidson's desk, and to this day many enthusiasts feel that the WG in the bike's model designation is in honor of his name, not Wide Glide. Whatever—the bike was such a hit that Harley-Davidson has brought the model back more than once since 1980. Which brings up another interesting point: perhaps the biggest corporate blunder occurred one year after the Wide Glide model bowed, when AMF sold their sinking motorcycle company to 13 brave souls. The rest, as we know, is history.

SPECIFICATIONS

Engine Displacement:	80 cubic inches
Weight:	644 pounds
Wheels:	21 inches front, 16 inches rear
Brakes:	Dual discs front, single disc rear

LORE

- Willie G. Davidson was among the 13 investors who bought Harley-Davidson Motor Company in 1981.
- The FXWG's Shovelhead engine produced about 67 horsepower.

2006 FXDI35 35TH ANNIVERSARY SUPER GLIDE®

Even though the 2006 35th Anniversary Super Glide model paid tribute to the past by acknowledging the 1971 FX for what it was—a landmark bike—the '06 model gave Harley enthusiasts a peek into the future as well. Owners of the red, white, and blue Super Glide model, like all other Dyna owners for that year, shifted gears through a new six-speed Cruise Drive transmission. All other Harley models would have to wait until 2007 for their six-packs: the Dyna was the only platform thus equipped. Other improvements included 49mm-diameter fork legs, a stronger swingarm for a wider 160/70x17 rear tire, internal oil lines from tank to engine, an automatic primary chain tensioner, reduced clutch lever pull, and electronic fuel injection as standard equipment. Cook Neilson, *Cycle* magazine's iconic editor during the 1970s, rode an Anniversary Super Glide motorcycle to Milwaukee for an article that appeared in the January 2006 issue of *Cycle World* magazine. He wrote of his experience: "In sixth gear at 70 mph, the Super Glide is plenty smooth enough; above or below that there's a bit of quaking and tingling, which Harley-Davidson is aware of and which Harley-Davidson considers an important part of the experience."

SPECIFICATIONS

Engine Displacement:	88 cubic inches
Transmission:	6-speed
Weight:	645 pounds
Seat Height:	26.8 inches

LORE

- Records show that 3,500 35th Anniversary Super Glide motorcycles were produced.
- The 1971 FX weighed 565 pounds.

Super Glide FX.
Call it the night train.

New 1200cc Super Glide FX. Ultimate superbike. The action-eager muscle machine that says move out 74-inch engine for blinding performance. Big-inch power with Sportster-like styling. Stripped, long-travel fork. Trouble-free Bendix carburetor, high-output alternator. And cast, polished covers. One look tells you you're the man for this hot new muscle machine. Super Glide FX. The night train. From Harley-Davidson. Number one where it counts . . . on the road and in the records. AMF | HARLEY-DAVIDSON, Milwaukee, Wisconsin 53201.

the Harley-Davidson outperformers

2006 FXDBI DYNA®
STREET BOB

Today Harley-Davidson considers bikes like the Street Bob model part of its Dark Custom movement. In 2006 the Street Bob motorcycle was actually just another model in the Dyna line, however, that was to change because the newest Bob wore some pretty rebellious colors. Specifically, Harley-Davidson referred to the Street Bob model's new paint colors as Black Denim, which in reality was a semigloss black. But the dull finish, coupled with the solo saddle, said it all—this bike was for the mainstream rebel and a blank canvas for a new brand of personalization that is vintage inspired and embraces minimalism. The Street Bob motorcycle was just a made-over Dyna model. And that was good, because this twin-shock model represents the blue-collar workers of America. Nothing fancy about this bike, just a genuine statement, stripped down and approachable. Even so, the Street Bob model's bobbed fenders, apehanger handlebar, staggered exhausts, solo seat, and of course the denim paint, told everybody that this was a bike for Harley's more rebellious customers. Welcome to the world of the Street Bob motorcycle. Welcome to the world of what would soon become known as Dark Custom line.

SPECIFICATIONS

Engine Displacement:	88 cubic inches
Weight:	634 pounds
Wheelbase:	64.2 inches
Seat Height:	25.8 inches

LORE

• The Street Bob model had a solo saddle; all other Dyna models had two-up seats.

• Harley's new denim colors first appeared on the Street Bob model.

2008 FXDF FAT BOB®

Buoyed by the sales success of the Street Bob model, Harley-Davidson went back to the Bob board in search of another approach to this minimalist concept. The result was the Fat Bob, what amounted to a Dyna in Fat Boy clothing. Practically everything about the Fat Bob model lends to the name. The tires and wheels are fat, the bobbed fenders are fat, the handlebar is fat, the Tommy Gun exhausts are fat, the rear shock absorbers are fat, even the 5.1-gallon gas tank and its instrument insert looks fat. The bike is fat on color combinations, too, with seven paint schemes available to customers. Perhaps the most striking was the Crimson Red Denim, but truth is the Fat Bob motorcycle looks so pure and spot-on that practically any color would look good. In the words of *Cycle World*, "The main performance question with any Harley-Davidson is, 'Do I look good on it?' The answer with Fat Bob is, 'It looks so right, I *feel* good on it.'"

SPECIFICATIONS

Engine Displacement:	96 cubic inches
Weight:	669 pounds
Wheelbase:	63.8 inches
Seat Height:	26.1 inches

LORE

- Original Fat Bob motorcycles were available with forward or mid foot controls.
- The Fat Bob model's front and rear tire sizes are 130/90x16 and 180/70x16 respectively.

2008 FXDC DYNA SUPER GLIDE® CUSTOM

It's time to get back to the basics of biking, and for that we can turn to the Dyna Super Glide Custom model, because it is the most basic of the Big Twins: there's nothing fancy about it. Simply, the Dyna Super Glide Custom model is a good, solid, all-around motorcycle that rewards its owner with a pleasurable ride no matter what the road conditions. This Dyna model can handle them all—traffic-congested city streets, meandering back roads, or long and boring stretches of interstate. Regardless of where you ride, the Dyna motorcycle serves up a comfortable ride so that you always feel confident about the next mile. In terms of features, the Custom actually is a rather straightforward model with laced spoke wheels, a single disc on each wheel, mid foot controls, a handlebar with a rather traditional bend to it, and a two-passenger saddle that dips to a relatively low 26.8 inches off the pavement. There's a reason that vanilla is the preferred flavor of ice cream among Americans, and there's a reason the Dyna Super Glide Custom model is favored by so many Harley enthusiasts in search of an affordable, reliable ride.

SPECIFICATIONS

Engine Displacement:	96 cubic inches
Weight:	645 pounds
Wheelbase:	64.2 inches
Seat Height:	26.8 inches

LORE

- The Custom shares its DNA with the first Super Glide model of 1971.
- Ample chrome-plated components lend to the Custom's name.

2010 DYNA® WIDE GLIDE®

The flamed paint job on the 1980 Dyna Wide Glide model—the original—is iconic. But that wild orange-on-black paint scheme was labor-intensive, requiring seven steps for its application. Thirty years later, when Harley-Davidson brought back the Wide Glide model, it did so with a near-duplicate paint scheme, but with one major difference: the 2010 colors were applied as an ultra-thin decal that was covered with clear coat. The new Wide Glide model also shared many of the same proportions as the original, something important to Willie G. Davidson, who was instrumental in producing both bikes. "Proportion," stressed Willie G., "is the main criteria to motorcycle design." Willie G. also noted something else about this bike: "It's not so much what's chromed, but how much of it appears on the bike," he said. Which explains the Wide Glide model's black rims with chromed spokes, not to mention a few other choice non-chromed components that simply add to the 2010 Dyna Wide Glide motorcycle's cool proportions.

SPECIFICATIONS

Engine Displacement:	96 cubic inches
Weight:	647 pounds
Fuel Capacity:	4.7 gallons
Seat Height:	25.5 inches

LORE

- With a 36-degree total fork angle, the Wide Glide model has the most radical stance of the Dyna line.
- For a clean look, the handlebar cables are routed internally.

2012 SUPER GLIDE® CUSTOM

From wheel to wheel, the Super Glide Custom® is a chromed-out feast for the eyes. Virtually every surface is chromed, polished, or painted to perfection. The machined cooling fin tips and chrome rocker covers of its 96-cubic-inch air-cooled Twin Cam 96 V-twin engine highlight the customization that gives this machine its name. Lustrous chrome surrounds the classic tank-mounted gauges, and the pullback handlebars are crafted from solid stainless steel. Polished fuel tank medallions and battery box cover make this machine seem like a one-of-a-kind custom ride, even though it is one of Harley-Davidson's least expensive Big Twins.

SPECIFICATIONS

Seat Height:	26.3 inches
Ground Clearance:	4.7 inches
Fuel Capacity:	5 gallons
Fuel Economy:	43 miles per gallon

LORE

- The Super Glide was the first factory-produced custom motorcycle.
- The Super Glide Custom is the most well-appointed of any Super Glide model.

2013 FXDB STREET BOB

Harley-Davidson's Street Bob was one of the first members of the Motor Company's Dark Custom line of bikes. It's also one of the most popular, and with good reason: its sleek, simple, cut-down custom look is exactly what many motorcyclists want in a motorcycle. A V-twin engine, minimal bodywork, two wheels, a place to sit, and a frame to hold the whole thing together: what more do you need? How about some Hard Candy Big Red Flake paint? Perfect.

SPECIFICATIONS

Price:	$12,999–$13,729
Fuel Capacity:	4.7 gallons
Bore:	3.75 inches
Stroke:	4.38 inches

LORE

- The Street Bob model reflected the popularity of "bobber" styling among motorcycle enthusiasts.
- The Street Bob model capitalized on the growing popularity of the Dyna models.

CHAPTER EIGHT

CIVILIZED CHOPPERS: THE SOFTAIL® MODELS

Who would have thought that a couple of industrious, and somewhat creative, custom bike builders in St. Louis, Missouri, could hit upon a frame design that would have such a major impact on the entire cruiser-bike market? By positioning two shock absorbers underneath the seat, parallel and horizontal to the ground, they came up with what would become the Softail frame.

Harley-Davidson's research and development team saw the potential in the frame's design and quickly bought rights to it, modifying the idea by placing the shocks beneath the transmission. And then they went to work, doing their magic to make the concept feasible in application and in production costs.

Coincidentally, at about that same time 13 other industrious and creative men went out on a financial limb to buy the Harley-Davidson Motor Company from its owners in 1981. Among the first orders of business tended to by that baker's dozen was the development of the Softail chassis and an all-new Big Twin engine that would become known as the V2 Evolution. The rest, as they say, is history.

1985 MODEL FXST SOFTAIL®

The FXST Softail changed the motorcycle industry practically overnight, establishing a new standard for what cruisers should look like, and also how they should ride and sound. The key word is *sound*; before too long the people who created Harley's advertisements had zeroed in on a phrase—"Potato-potato-potato"—that captured the essence of the American-made V-twin engine's sound as it cruised along the great American boulevard. And after the FXST's engine noise got the attention of bystanders, they feasted their eyes on a bike that looked very much like a custom chopper. But beneath the bad-boy styling that took its cues from the venerable hardtail frame was a revolutionary chassis, complete with hidden rear suspension.

SPECIFICATIONS

Engine Displacement:	80 cubic inches
Weight:	618 pounds
Wheelbase:	66.3 inches
Wheels and Tires:	21/16 inches

LORE

- The Softail frame was developed by a couple of custom motorcycle builders in Missouri.
- The Softail was the first all-new model to use the V2 Evolution engine.

2005 SOFTAIL® SPRINGER® CLASSIC

You'll be excused if you mistakenly take the 2005 Softail Springer Classic model for a vintage motorcycle, because that was the goal of Harley-Davidson stylists when they created it. True, the disc brake and belt drive remind us that this is a modern-day model, but look past that and you'll notice that the Classic's basic lines and styling cues are—how shall we put this?—classic. The front end suggests 1948 and earlier vintage, those 16-inch balloon tires echo that image, and by now every Harley aficionado associates that softly sprung Softail frame with the cool-looking rigid frames used by the Motor Company right up through 1957. Want more? Okay, the exhaust system mimics the pipes of old, and check out the art deco stainless steel band and classic (there's that word again) name badge on the gas tank and on the side of the oil bag. Anyone who appreciates motorcycle heritage will warm to the Softail Springer Classic model. And people who don't maintain a romantic link to the past just might change their minds once they look closely at this timeless modern-day classic.

SPECIFICATIONS

Engine Displacement:	88 cubic inches
Weight:	731 pounds
Wheelbase:	64.5 inches
Seat Height:	27.4 inches

LORE

• The emblems on the oil tank are replicas of those found on Knuckleheads.

• Harley's Parts & Accessories division offered vintage-style leather saddlebags for the Classic.

2006 FXSTI
SOFTAIL® STANDARD

You can't help but feel like a freewheeling chopper rider when you swing a leg over the Softail Standard model's slim saddle to blast down the boulevard. Despite its nondescript name, all the things about this bike point toward it being a chopper. The bold look begins with the bike's overall stance, determined by a pair of raked triple trees that set overall fork angle at a radical 33.5 degrees. Plant a pullback handlebar on top of the triple tree, bolt a set of forward-mounted foot controls onto the frame's downtubes, and dress the bike with a low-profile seat that reaches back to the bobbed rear fender and you begin to get the picture. The staggered individual exhausts add to the scenario, and of course every chopper must have a 21-inch front tire that's complemented by a huge 16-inch rear. And if you look at that 16-incher from the back you'll see a big chunk of rubber staring back at you, because the 2006 Standard's rear footprint is 200mm wide. Captain America and Billy, step aside. The Softail Standard is coming through, and it's bringing with it a whole new standard for today's chopper rider.

SPECIFICATIONS

Engine Displacement:	88 cubic inches
Weight:	651 pounds
Wheelbase:	66.9 inches
Seat Height:	25.2 inches

LORE

• The 200mm rear tire was new on all Softail models for 2006.

• Harley-Davidson also reintroduced the Softail Heritage model in 2006.

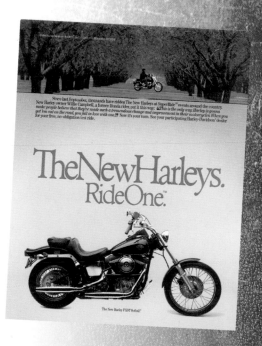

2007 FLSTN
SOFTAIL® DELUXE

Harley-Davidson stylists used an old trick to create a new model for 2005. By mixing a few nostalgia-laden components into the popular Softail Heritage platform, they came up with one of the most elegant models ever—the Softail Deluxe. Perhaps Bill Davidson, Harley's director of marketing at the time, said it best: "With the Softail line Harley-Davidson has always sought to combine a classic motorcycle profile with innovative mechanical design and technology that makes these models as comfortable and capable as they are beautiful." The Softail Deluxe model fills that description to a T. Its credentials include liberal use of the chrome plating that makes any Harley-Davidson motorcycle stand out, classic wide whitewall tires on nostalgic laced-spoke rims, a plush seat that sets the rider low to the pavement, and colorful paint options. And it all adds up to an eye-catching Softail model. The Deluxe offered something else—ergonomics that were especially friendly to shorter riders. And like all 2007 models, the Deluxe received a 96-cubic-inch engine and Cruise Drive six-speed transmission that elevated its performance to a new level.

SPECIFICATIONS

Engine Displacement:	96 cubic inches
Fuel Capacity:	5 gallons
Weight:	695 pounds
Seat Height:	24.5 inches

LORE

• The seat height for the Deluxe is a full inch lower than that of the Heritage Softail Classic model.

• Like the Springer Classic model, the Deluxe has a tombstone taillight.

2008 FXCW ROCKER™ C

Interestingly, the Rocker owes its origins to supply and demand. When the Harley-Davidson market began to explode under high customer demand during the 1990s, the fallout was a host of small companies offering turnkey customs powered by air-cooled V-twin engines. The bikes they built helped fill the void left by the shortage of new Harley-Davidson motorcycles, and the cottage industry flourished. Harley's marketing department recognized the potential for a similar model in the Motor Company's lineup, leading to the Rocker model. The model checks in with chopper-like proportions, too: a fork angle of 37.5 degrees that lends to the bike's overall length of 95 inches, a 240mm rear tire, and a low seat height. The Rocker C's solo seat has a foldout assembly beneath it to allow two-up riding.

SPECIFICATIONS

Engine Displacement:	96 cubic inches
Weight:	686 pounds
Wheelbase:	69.2 inches
Seat Height:	25.25 inches

LORE

- The "Trick" stowaway seat wasn't offered on the standard Rocker (with a seat height of 24.5 inches) model.
- The Rocker C model also had more chrome trim than the standard Rocker.

PASS IT ALONG

IF YOU desire to avoid accidents, arrests and lawsuits, and do not wish to make enemies for motorcycling, or provoke the passage of onerous laws

Keep Your Muffler Closed

except when steep hills or heavy roads are encountered; there rarely is real necessity for opening the muffler cut-out at any other time. Also observe all the rules of the road at all times, always keeping in mind the rights of the other road users; and finally dress and act like a gentleman.

G. B. GIBSON, Sec.-Treas., F. A. M.,
Lock Box 947, Westboro, Mass.

℃ The Federation of American Motorcyclists has done a lot of good work for "the cause" since its organization in 1903, and is looking out for your interests all the time. Please do all you can to help us in the good work, by becoming a member, continuing a member, and inducing others to become members.

2008 FLSTSB SOFTAIL® CROSS BONES®

Harley-Davidson's Dark Custom movement really crystalized with the Cross Bones model. During the bike's unveiling Willie G. Davidson first used the words to describe the new Softail bike, and since that time various other models have been added to form the Dark Custom DNA. The Cross Bones model's formula is rather straightforward. Begin with the Softail platform, include a few bobber-inspired components, such as the bobbed front and rear fenders, springer front end with apehanger handlebar, staggered shotgun-style exhaust pipes, half-moon footboards, a Fat Bob gas tank, and a solo tractor-style seat, and you get a clearer picture of what a Dark Custom model represents. Naturally you'll top it with a dark, wicked color—black always works for a bike like this—highlighted with traditional pinstriping, and you have the Cross Bones model. No doubt, this Dark Custom motorcycle has shed new light on the direction that Harley-Davidson intends to take some of its future models.

SPECIFICATIONS

Engine Displacement:	96 cubic inches
Weight:	700 pounds
Wheelbase:	64.5 inches
Seat Height:	26.6 inches

LORE

- The Cross Bones model was introduced midyear during a special ceremony at the Viper Room on Hollywood's Sunset Strip.
- Detachable accessories were immediately available for the Cross Bones model.

2010 FAT BOY® LO

Ever since it joined the Harley-Davidson family in 1990, the Fat Boy model has been a favorite among Softail customers. The bike sported valance fenders and disk wheels that made it easily recognizable on the street, and who can forget the Fat Boy model's role in the movie *Terminator 2: Judgment Day*? But after two faithful decades the aging model needed a boost, or in this case, a drop. A second Fat Boy model was added in 2010, called the Fat Boy Lo. As the name implies, the Lo has a low seat height. The updated Softail model also received a new, narrower handlebar, and the combination makes the rider feel more like he or she is riding in the bike rather than on it. A few other special styling features, among them the half-moon footboards and painted fork tins and wheel centers, help distance the Fat Boy Lo's styling even further from the original Fat Boy Lo model.

SPECIFICATIONS

Engine Displacement:	96 cubic inches
Weight:	700 pounds
Wheelbase:	64.5 inches
Seat Height:	24.3 inches

LORE

- The Fat Boy Lo's seat is lower and narrower than the standard Fat Boy model's.
- The 2005 Fat Boy model was offered as a 15th Anniversary model.

2011 HERITAGE SOFTAIL® CLASSIC

What we have here is truly a classic in more than name only. Even though the Heritage Softail model has been in the lineup since 1986, the fact remains that its styling is timeless. That shouldn't surprise Harley aficionados, either, because from the get-go this bike was intended to mimic the early Panhead. Indeed, when the Heritage Softail model first came out, people from Harley-Davidson's marketing staff described it as representing New Nostalgia. The phrase never caught on with the motorcycle press, but the Heritage Softail model certainly did with customers, and this retro-style bike sporting a timeless look has been one of the best-selling models ever since. And how can you resist its splendid lines, which pay homage to Harley-Davidson's storied heritage? Graceful fenders and balloon tires, the tri-bar running lights with detachable windscreen up front, and studded leather-like saddlebags set the theme for a bike that suggests a ride from another time. Say, 1949 . . .

SPECIFICATIONS

Engine Displacement:	96 cubic inches
Weight:	730 pounds
Wheelbase:	64.5 inches
Seat Height:	25.5 inches

LORE

• The original Heritage Softail Special model weighed less than 700 pounds.

• MSRP for the original was under $10,000.

2011 SOFTAIL® DELUXE

Like all the models powered by the Big Twin engine, the Softail Deluxe received the 96-cubic-inch upgrade in 2007. Along with the engine came the Cruise Drive six-speed transmission, making for a smooth-running package. But other than those upgrades and new paint color options, not much else was changed on the Softail Deluxe model over the years. That is a credit to its styling, making it one of the more colorful models in the lineup.

SPECIFICATIONS

Engine Displacement:	96 cubic inches
Weight:	695 pounds
Wheelbase:	64.5 inches
Seat Height:	24.5 inches

LORE

- Custom colors were available for the Softail Deluxe and the Heritage Softail Classic models.
- Fuel mileage for the FL Softail models was rated at 54 mpg highway and 35 mpg city.

2012 SOFTAIL® BLACKLINE®

Harley-Davidson designed the Blackline to be the essence of motorcycling; its clean look, simplified profile, and defiant attitude are meant to embrace the pure essence of riding. Designers used minimal tank graphics to emphasize the presence of the massive Twin Cam 103 V-Twin engine. A split drag-style handlebar with the speedometer bolted directly to the triple clamp adds to the minimalist appearance of Blackline. The design team kept things clean and simple in the back too. A 144mm rear tire tucked under a chopped, black fender and wrapped around a gloss black rim stick to the purposeful motif.

SPECIFICATIONS

Seat Height:	24 inches
Ground Clearance:	5.25 inches
Lean Angle (Right):	24.4 degrees
Lean Angle (Left):	25.9 degrees

LORE

• Harley-Davidson designed the Blackline to capture the pure essence of riding.

• Every aspect of the Blackline, from its split drag bars to its cut-down rear fender, was designed to emphasize the functional aspect of the machine.

2013 SOFTAIL SLIM

With the Softail Slim, Harley-Davidson designers recreated the look of a cut-down Panhead Hydra-Glide bobber. They didn't overlook a single detail. Take the instrument console, a sculpted "cat-eye" design that would look right at home on the tank of a 1940s-era Panhead or Knucklehead. The fact that it's finished in black rather than chrome is a nod to the first bikes built after World War II was over. That was a time when raw materials were in short supply and many parts that had been plated in nickel, cadmium, or chromium were painted black out of necessity.

SPECIFICATIONS

Price:	$15,699–$16,099
Rake:	31 degrees
Trail:	5.8 inches
Weight:	671 pounds

LORE

• With a dry weight of just 671 pounds, the Slim came by its name honestly.

• The Slim proved just what a versatile design the original Softail chassis was.

CHAPTER NINE
SETTING THE RECORD:
THE RACE BIKES

Other than a few exceptional years, Harley-Davidson Motor Company has always fielded race teams. Why spend valuable money and corporate resources on bikes that are meant to simply chase a trophy? Lots of reasons, really, but perhaps Harley's most famous race team manager of all time, the late Dick O'Brien, said it best: "We race so that our customers have a place to ride to." That's good enough for most Harley enthusiasts, but there's really more to this picture.

Harley-Davidson also competes at the national level to develop, improve, and promote its products. The V-Rod motorcycle traces its roots to the VR1000 superbike program, and the XR1200X model

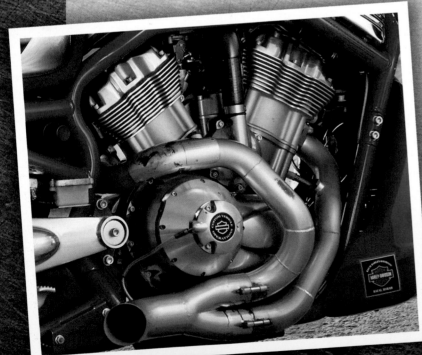

owes its styling and graphics to the much-fabled XR750 flat-track racer. And at the drag strip the Screamin' Eagle colors are displayed on the Vance & Hines Pro Stock racer that is based on the V-Rod model.

There's much more, but the fact remains that ever since Walter Davidson won an endurance run in 1908, the folks in Milwaukee have placed high value on competing on the race-tracks of America. So, does competition improve the breed? If you ask Harley owners, they'll probably tell you that it does. And if they don't know for sure, they can always ride their bikes to the racetrack to see for themselves.

1921 MODEL 221
8-VALVE RACER

Racing technology was in its infancy when Harley-Davidson showed up at the racetrack with its 8-Valve Racer in 1916. Harley-Davidson engineers produced a bike capable of speeds in excess of 110 miles per hour. Chief among their modifications was the steel plate cradle, which was spliced into the frame rails at the base of the engine, and a reinforced backbone to hold the gas and oil tanks. The springer fork with friction dampers and the seat's two springs was the bike's only suspension. There was no transmission, so power to the wheel was direct from the engine. Early racers had no brakes; once the rider got up to top speed, slowing down presented a challenge.

SPECIFICATIONS

Engine Displacement:	60 cubic inches
Compression Ratio:	6:1
Weight:	275 pounds
Wheelbase:	51.5 inches

LORE

• Otto Walker and Ralph Hepburn set numerous speed records in 1921 aboard the 8-valver.

• The 8-Valve Racer was priced at $1,500 to discourage privateers from buying it.

OTTO WALKER ON HARLEY-DAVIDSON EIGHT VALVE MACHINE WHICH AVERAGED 104.43 M.P.H. IN 25 MILE RACE AT BEVERLY, CALIFORNIA, APRIL 24, 1921

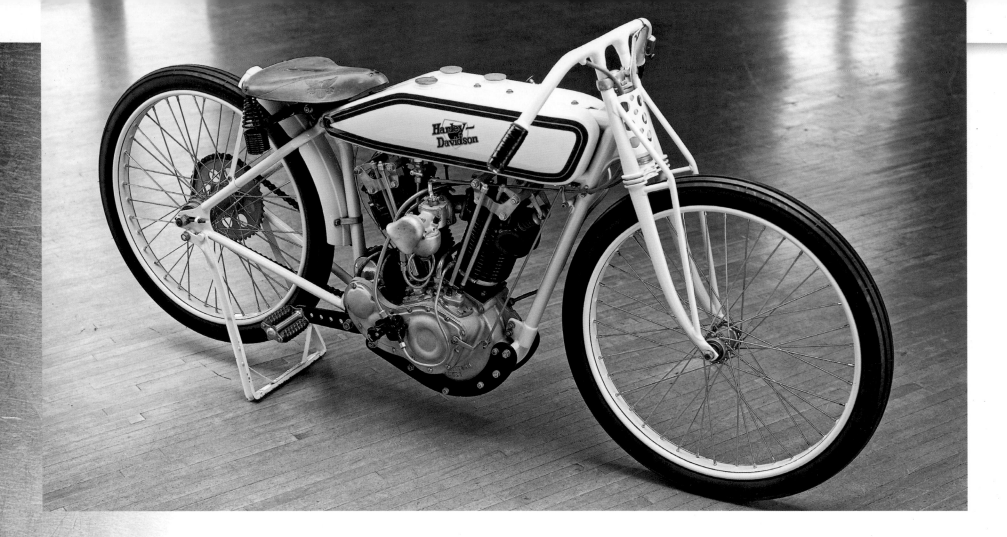

1924 8-VALVE RACER

It's disputed exactly when the name "Wrecking Crew" was applied to Harley-Davidson's juggernaut racing team, but it pops up in literature dating back to the teens. Harley's factory race team was a dominant force during that era. Riders like Ralph Hepburn, Jim Davis, Fred Ludlow, Maldwyn Jones, Otto Walker, Walter Higley, and Ray Weishaar raced their Harley motorcycles to fame and glory on the dirt ovals and board tracks that populated the landscape. In 1921 Walker was the first rider to win a race with an average speed more than 100 miles per hour, and later that year Hepburn won at Dodge City, Kansas. After several accidents that took the lives of spectators and racers alike, board-track racing was banned.

SPECIFICATIONS

Engine Displacement:	60 cubic inches
Horsepower:	About 15 horsepower
Wheels:	28-inch diameter
Number Produced:	30-50

LORE

• The 8-Valve engine's rocker arms were not covered.

• A total-loss lubrication system dumped the oil onto the track.

1926 MODEL S
"PEASHOOTER"

The name "Peashooter" came from the "pop-pop-pop" sound the single-cylinder engine exhaust made. The company derived this racing motor from production pieces starting in the early 1920s to meet the rules for a new national racing championship class under 350cc (21.35 cubic inches) that commenced in 1926. The regular production 21.1-cubic-inch A and B singles fit this displacement limitation perfectly. An effective dual-port cylinder head improved breathing over the stock production singles in Harley-Davidson's lineup. Bosch developed a compact magneto, nicknamed "the Baby," for ignition.

SPECIFICATIONS

Engine Displacement:	21 cubic inches
Number of cylinders:	1
Brakes:	None
Rear Suspension:	Rigid

LORE

- The Model S was designed to compete in the AMA's 21-cubic-inch racing class.
- The Model S earned the name "Peashooter" for the popping sound of its exhaust.

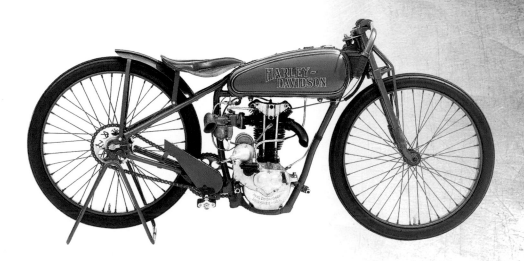

WR RACER

In 1933 AMA Class C racing rules called for race bikes based on production models, so Harley-Davidson developed the WR, based on the 45-cubic-inch engine side-valve Model WL. Soon WR racers were going head to head with riders on Indian's venerable Scout. The classic Harley-Indian wars raged for years. Racers campaigned their WR bikes well into the 1950s, and not until the KR officially replaced the WR in 1952 did the top riders consider trading in their bikes. Indeed, Joe Leonard, the first racer to win the AMA Grand National Championship under the season-long format instituted in 1954, was reluctant to trade in his fast and reliable WR for the new, unproven KR during his first championship season.

SPECIFICATIONS

Engine Displacement:	45 cubic inches
Horsepower:	About 40 horsepower
Transmission:	3-speed
Weight:	About 300 pounds

LORE

- Billy Huber (WR) and Bobby Hill (Indian Scout) finished in a dead heat for first at the 1948 Atlanta National.
- Jimmy Chann won the Springfield Mile—and the AMA Number One Plate—aboard a WR in 1947, 1948, and 1949.

KRTT

Like the WR, the KR came in many variations, among them the KRTT developed for TT Steeplechase racing and road racing. The wide-open racing on the dirt ovals was left to the KR, although all models were based on the K Model, which replaced the WL in 1952 as Harley-Davidson's 45-incher for the street. And the KR engine was clearly a race engine, boasting hotter camshafts, higher compression ratio, ball-bearing mains, magneto ignition, a larger carburetor, and an open exhaust system. The combination was especially successful on road racers like the one shown here. The KRTT was especially proven on the asphalt courses, winning to the very end, when Cal Rayborn accomplished back-to-back wins at the Daytona 200 in 1968 and 1969. The example shown here with a rear disc brake and front drum brake is similar to the bike that Rayborn won with in 1969. The following year Harley-Davidson replaced the side-valve KR with the new overhead-valve XR750, and another page of racing history was turned.

SPECIFICATIONS

Engine Displacement:	45 cubic inches
Transmission:	4-speed
Oil Capacity:	6 quarts
Wheelbase:	54 inches

LORE

• Carroll Resweber won his four straight AMA Grand National Championships with a KR.

• The KRTT was the first Harley-Davidson racer to have rear suspension.

1977 MX 250

What's this, a two-stroke *motocross* bike dressed in Harley-Davidson livery? And it was made in Italy? Well, yes, that's right, the MX 250 was a product of the Aermacchi plant, and it was produced at a time when the motorcycle industry was experiencing phenomenal growth. Motorcycle companies weren't quite sure where the industry was headed, so the basic solution was to offer as many models as possible so that your brand would gain as big a portion of the pie as possible. And so Harley-Davidson—owned by AMF at the time—joined the motocross party with this quarter-liter racer. The bike was surprisingly fast, too, leading the editors of *Hot Bike* magazine to state in their February 1978 issue, "In terms of throttle response, the highly tuned Harley-Davidson displays dramatic bursts of power when the throttle is tugged open. As a matter of fact, it might seem more appropriate that this motorcycle have a trigger instead of a throttle. Wheelspin is very easy to induce in any gear, provided the peaky power plant is within its rather narrow power band . . . the H-D is not what you'd call a beginner's machine." A factory prepared MX 250 was campaigned in the AMA National and Supercross series by "Rocket" Rex Staten.

SPECIFICATIONS

Engine Displacement:	15 cubic inches (250cc)
Weight:	248 pounds
Wheelbase:	57.5 inches
Seat Height:	37 inches

LORE

- In 1978 *Hot Bike* magazine was a general-interest publication; today it's exclusively for American V-twins.
- The MX 250's fuel tank was made of aluminum.

2006 V-ROD® DESTROYER®

The V-Rod Destroyer motorcycle is not for sissies. Harley-Davidson made only a handful of them (it's been reported that fewer than 500 were built), and all Destroyer bikes went to certified drag racers who were to compete in spec classes promoted by various drag-racing organizations. While the Destroyer model is based on a stock V-Rod, it is, pure and simple, a production bike that can unleash hell on its rider's command. Its stroker engine cranks out enough horsepower to propel the 510-pound projectile through the standing quarter-mile in about 9.3 seconds with a terminal speed of over 150 mph. While the horsepower lurches and bites the asphalt through the huge rear drag slick, the wheelie bar on the back helps keep the front tire on the pavement. An electric shift button ensures quick, positive shifting of gears through the Andrews Products reinforced five-speed transmission, and the special exhaust pipe is ceramic-coated. So what's it like to ride down the 1,320-foot Armco gauntlet? Here's what *Cycle World's* Mark Hoyer had to say in his report: "It's like walking on tiptoes to the brink of Armageddon. It's louder than hell, you're not sure what's in your near future, you're wondering about your past, and nothing happens until everything happens and you are hurled into the abyss at nearly 2g's."

SPECIFICATIONS

Engine Displacement:	76 cubic inches (1300cc)
Compression Ratio:	14.5:1
Weight:	510 pounds
Rear Tire:	25 x7x18-inch drag slick

LORE

• The V-Rod Destroyer model sold for about $31,000.
• Mark Hoyer's best run was a 9.783 at 133.88 mph.

SCREAMIN' EAGLE
PERFORMANCE PARTS

Quality power that works.
Screamin' Eagle high-performance parts are engineered to work with stock parts and with other Screamin' Eagle accessories. Designed, tested and built to Harley-Davidson's rigid specifications by the people who know Harleys best. For quality parts and quality power, look to Screamin' Eagle.

CHAPTER TEN

MODERN MUSCLE: THE V-RODS

If motorcycles truly had DNA, then we would see that the V-Rod is either a mutant strain or a whole different species, for it is a Harley-Davidson like no other. The liquid-cooled engine's specs alone suggest that this bike is in no way related to any of its air-cooled counterparts. Consider that the included cylinder angle is 60 degrees, compared to the Big Twin's institutionalized 45 degrees. Each of the V-Rod model's cylinders has double overhead camshafts that operate four valves per cylinder. Indeed, none of the V-Rod model's drivetrain components are interchangeable with the other Harley

models' mechanicals, and we don't even have to talk about how the V-Rod model's beauty lines match with the other Milwaukee-bred bikes.

Yet the V-Rod model is as much a Harley-Davidson as any of the other bikes that wear the famous Bar & Shield logo. Some of its development can be traced back to Harley-Davidson's VR1000 superbike project of the 1990s. Moreover, like all Harley-Davidson motorcycles sold in this country, the V-Rod is made in America. And that, ladies and gentlemen, is reason enough to include it in the family.

2003 V-ROD®

In 2002, one year before Harley-Davidson celebrated its 100th anniversary by building bikes with special paint and badges (as shown on the 2003 V-Rod pictured above) and throwing the biggest party the city of Milwaukee had ever seen, the Motor Company introduced the first liquid-cooled production bike in the company's century-long history: the 2002 VRSCA V-Rod. The V-Rod model was also the most powerful motorcycle Harley had ever built. The V-Rod model's sixty-degree four-valve 1120-cc V-twin cranked out 115 horsepower, helping the most American of motorcycle manufacturers wind down its first century with a bang instead of a whimper.

SPECIFICATIONS

Engine Displacement:	69 cubic inches (1130cc)
Weight:	596 pounds
Wheelbase:	67.5 inches
Seat Height:	26 inches

LORE

- The original V-Rod model's bare metal finish required special cleaning products to keep the shiny parts shiny.
- As with the aborted Nova project, Harley tapped the technical expertise of Porsche when engineering the liquid-cooled engine.

2005 V-ROD®

Within a few years' time the V-Rod had established its niche in Harley-Davidson's family of bikes. Owners who were impressed with the liquid-cooled engine's performance embraced the new model with the understanding that they had the best-performing model in Harley's lineup. For some V-Rod owners, however, the novelty of owning this unorthodox V-twin wore off and they quietly sold their bikes to return to the air-cooled ranks. Either way, customers were happy, and the V-Rod model was no longer looked upon as an oddity; rather, it was seen as an alternative to the traditional models that wore the famous Bar & Shield logo. The V-Rod model established a reputation as a high-performance model among non-Harley enthusiasts as well. Perhaps the high point came when, in the March 2002 issue of *Cycle World* magazine, the V-Rod model won a shootout between four performance cruisers. Clearly the V-Rod model's claimed 115 horsepower at the crankshaft was more than marketing bluster—this bike's engine was the real deal, and soon enough the performance aftermarket thrived on developing go-fast items for this power cruiser. But the best was yet to come for V-Rod owners.

SPECIFICATIONS

Engine Displacement:	69 cubic inches (1130cc)
Weight:	596 pounds
Wheelbase:	67.5 inches
Seat Height:	26 inches

LORE

- The 2002 V-Rod model won a four-bike shootout in the March 2002 issue of *Cycle World* magazine.
- Initial development of the Revolution engine was conducted by Porsche Engineering in Germany.

2006 VRSCR STREET ROD®

What is a Street Rod motorcycle? Harley-Davidson stated in its 2006 advertising literature that a Street Rod was a "new roadster-inspired ride with 120 horses, 40 degrees worth of lean, steep rake, mid-mount foot controls and an inverted front fork." *IronWorks* magazine proclaimed, "The bike is, in a word, fantastic." One editor for *American Iron* wrote that the Street Rod model is "a hybrid because it incorporates qualities from three different styles of motorcycles—part sportbike, part standard, part cruiser." Indeed, practically every magazine report supported the claim that this was the best-handling Harley-Davidson ever built up to that time. Yet, despite all the positive hype given the Street Rod bike, it never turned the corner in terms of sales, and within two years the best-handling Harley-Davidson motorcycle ever built was dropped like yesterday's Paris fashion. Even so, Street Rod owners today are reluctant to sell their bikes because they know that they own one of the most "fantastic" Harley models ever produced.

SPECIFICATIONS

Engine Displacement:	69 cubic inches (1130cc)
Weight:	618 pounds
Wheelbase:	66.7 inches
Seat Height:	30 inches

LORE

- *Cycle World* magazine's quarter-mile time for the Street Rod model was 11.80 seconds at 115.75 mph.
- The Street Rod model was unveiled to the motorcycle press in Southern California to take advantage of the nice country roads.

2007 VRSCDX NIGHT ROD® SPECIAL

By 2007 the VRSC family—now better known as the V-Rod family—had grown to five models. The latest entry was the VRSCDX Night Rod Special model. And special this bike was! Its low stance, blacked-out paint with fire-red graphics, and small handlebar fairing to pierce the night air set the tone for this power cruiser. There was also plenty of punch to be found in its 1130cc 60-degree liquid-cooled V-twin engine, which pounded out 120 horsepower to the crankshaft. But what really got everybody's attention was the Night Rod Special model's rear tire, a huge 240mm Dunlop that was the largest chunk of rubber ever wrapped around a factory-built Harley-Davidson wheel. If looks could kill, the Night Rod Special would certainly be on the Most Wanted list!

A LOT OF REVOLUTIONS START WITH BURNING TIRES.

It's a riot on the street all right, and there's a motorcycle behind it. A new mix of performance and pure Harley-Davidson custom. We call it the V-Rod motorcycle. Dragstrip-inspired styling. Our latest engine: the tire-smoking 115 horsepower Revolution V-Twin. In other words, the kind of movement we can all get behind. 1-800-443-2153 or www.harley-davidson.com. **The Legend Rolls On.**

SPECIFICATIONS

Engine Displacement:	69 cubic inches (1130cc)
Weight:	643 pounds
Wheelbase:	67 inches
Seat Height:	25.2 inches

LORE

- All 2007 V-Rod models received five-gallon fuel tanks.
- The V-Rod engine's redline is 9000 rpm.

2009 VRSCF V-ROD MUSCLE®

Before anyone on the assembly line so much as budged a muscle to begin production of the first V-Rod Muscle model, people in the Motor Company's styling division spent hours on Internet forums learning what visual cues V-Rod owners wanted on future models. They learned that the V-Rod needed to have angular, more aggressive lines. The result is the V-Rod Muscle, which one Harley-Davidson spokesman described as a bike with "*visual* mass, not mass." The V-Rod Muscle exudes the look of a muscle car from the early 1970s. The body panels are larger and bolder than before, the wheels seem to be chiseled out of hardened steel, and the squared seat suggests it's designed for drag racing rather than a leisurely cruise down the boulevard. Most of all, the exhaust system looks like it was hand-formed from raw steel tubing at the local speed shop and then routed on either side of the bike. Which brings up an interesting detail about the V-Rod Muscle—unlike its Big Twin cousins, the V-Rod Muscle model's left-side exhaust pipe originates from the front cylinder, while the right-side pipe loops out of the rear exhaust port. Finally, the big 240mm rear tire leaves a large footprint, as you'd expect from a bike named "Muscle".

SPECIFICATIONS

Engine Displacement:	76 cubic inches (1250cc)
Weight:	640 pounds
Wheelbase:	67 inches
Seat Height:	25.6 inches

LORE

- The larger 1250cc engine produced 86 lbs-ft of torque, more than 10 percent more than the 1130cc engine.
- The V-Rod Muscle model's gas tank is formed from sheet molded compound, the same material used to make Corvette bodies.

2011 NIGHT ROD® SPECIAL

The VRSC platform began its 10th year in 2011, by which time Harley-Davidson's marketing department had a handle on just what direction to take the bike in terms of its customer base. And that direction pointed towards more aggressive performance. To do that, the model lineup was whittled down to just a pair of sporty models—the V-Rod Muscle and the Night Rod Special. Both 2011 models were given minor styling changes, and both checked in with the potent 1250cc engine so that these power cruisers lived up to their names and reputations.

SPECIFICATIONS

Engine Displacement:	76 cubic inches (1250cc)
Weight:	643 pounds
Wheelbase:	67 inches
Seat Height:	25.2 inches

LORE

- Although known for its black or denim colors, the 2011 paint options included Chrome Yellow as shown here.

- The Night Rod Special model's engine cases are black; the V-Rod Muscle model's remained natural finish for 2011.

CHAPTER ELEVEN

BESPOKE BIKES:
CUSTOM VEHICLE OPERATIONS™

Owners of Custom Vehicle Operations (CVO) bikes don't subscribe to the "less is more" doctrine. They call a spade a spade, and for them, quite simply, more is more. In fact, considering all the accessories and modifications given to a typical CVO bike, you could honestly say that more is most, because for more money you get the most in terms of add-ons to the bike.

The first CVO models were offered in 1999, and their primary purpose was to help the production team seek ways to create new products effectively, efficiently, and economically. The program was such a success that the CVO concept became a Motor Company institution, and it's now a trend to offer four distinct, limited-number models each year.

But what hasn't changed is the concept of including as much bling on each bike as possible. The CVO team does that efficiently, too, and if you need proof just add up the cost of the individual items on a particular model and then compare that price to the bike's MSRP. And every time the comparison pencils out in favor of the CVO customer who gets most for more.

2002 FLHRSEI SCREAMIN' EAGLE® CVO™ ROAD KING®

Harley-Davidson dealers and customers across the country embraced the Screamin' Eagle CVO concept. The idea of equipping a bike as popular as the Road King model with custom and performance parts from the Screamin' Eagle accessory line appealed to owners who wanted the best. Perhaps the most welcomed Screamin' Eagle modification was to the Twin Cam 88 engine which, thanks to SE big-bore cylinders, checked in at 95 cubic inches. Of course, there were plenty of chromed and polished bolt-on accessories available to dress the Road King model, and the package was topped with a show-quality paint job.

SPECIFICATIONS

Engine Displacement:	95 cubic inches
Weight:	741 pounds
Wheelbase:	63.5 inches
Seat Height:	26.5 inches

LORE

- Screamin' Eagle 95-cubic-inch engines produced 95 lbs-ft of torque at 3500 rpm.
- The in-house code name for the CVO Road King model was Mad Dog.

2007 FXSTSSE
SCREAMIN' EAGLE® CVO™
SOFTAIL® SPRINGER

For a full understanding of what the Screamin' Eagle CVO line means, hear what one Harley-Davidson spokesman had to say when the 2007 line was unveiled: "We highlight the breadth and depth of the Parts & Accessories catalog with these bikes." Indeed they do, and that year's Softail Springer model is a prime example. Like the other three 2007 CVO models, the Softail Springer is powered by a 110-cubic-inch hot-rod engine that's based on the TC96, relying on big-bore cylinders and stroker flywheels to gain the additional 14 cubic inches. The big engine was rated at 105 lbs-ft of torque at 3000 rpm. The CVO model's chromed and polished cosmetic accessories are from the Centerline group, and three paint schemes include the hand-painted tribal graphics that were offered for the year. A special flush-fit smoke-tint taillight is tucked into the bobbed fender, and a 1.25-inch diameter handlebar is within easy reach of the rider.

SPECIFICATIONS

Engine Displacement:	110 cubic inches
Weight:	694 pounds
Wheelbase:	65.4 inches
Seat Height:	24.7 inches

LORE

- The 2007 CVO Softail Springer model had more than 50 accessories.
- The 2007 Parts & Accessories catalog contained 896 pages showcasing more than 13,000 part numbers.

2008 FXDSE2 SCREAMIN' EAGLE® CVO™ DYNA®

Even though the 2008 Screamin' Eagle CVO Dyna model shared the Pro Street styling theme with the model offered for 2007, it was in many ways a whole different bike. Some customers in 2007 complained that the CVO Dyna model felt too long: it was quite a stretch for riders less than six feet tall to comfortably reach the forward foot controls and the hand grips. And so, for 2008, the seat was moved slightly forward, and the front end sported an inverted fork that was slightly lower than the one offered the year before. But the CVO Dyna model still boasted all the bling and custom accessories found on the rest of the Screamin' Eagle line. There was much to be seen in the paint graphics, too. Each piece of the CVO Dyna model's body ware was hand-painted, and graphics were individually applied before the six to eight layers of clear coat were added to protect the colorful finish from nicks and scratches. In the purest sense, these paint jobs use custom applications to set them apart from any other on the market.

SPECIFICATIONS

Engine Displacement:	110 cubic inches
Transmission:	6-speed
Weight:	650 pounds
Wheelbase:	64.2 inches

LORE

- 2,600 CVO Dyna models were offered, of which 1,050 were serialized to commemorate Harley-Davidson's 105th anniversary.
- The 2008 CVO Dyna model's MSRP was $24,995.

2008 FLHRSE4 SCREAMIN' EAGLE® ROAD KING®

Bill Davidson, who was Vice President of Motorcycle Product Development in 2008, described the CVO division as a "place to show off new P&A [Parts & Accessories]." And the 2008 CVO Road King model rolled into the limelight with many new accessories and options, chief among them the new anti-lock braking system that was offered for the first time on Harley touring models. The "new" list also included front and rear brakes, a six-gallon fuel tank, an eye-catching tank console, a handlebar riser cover with indicator lights, mirrors, and a custom leather seat with backrests and saddlebags. And, like the rest of the touring line's standard models, the CVO Road King model had the new Isolated Drive System in the rear hub for smoother acceleration and shifting and the Electronic Throttle Control technology that eliminated one of the cables (the throttle cable) cluttering the handlebar.

I WANT YOU ON A HARLEY
SEE YOUR NEAREST HARLEY DEALER

SPECIFICATIONS

Engine Displacement:	110 cubic inches
Weight:	754 pounds
Wheelbase:	63 inches
Seat Height:	26.3 inches

LORE

- The frame and swingarm on the 2008 CVO Road King model are color-matched to the rest of the bike's paint scheme.
- Optional items include Ironside trim strips and Winder forged-aluminum wheels.

2009 FLTRSE CVO™ ROAD GLIDE®

If it's true that good things come in threes, then 2009 was a landmark year for the CVO line. It marked the third year for the 110-cubic-inch engine option, and for the third time in the same decade the CVO group included the Road Glide model. And—by coincidence?—Harley-Davidson offered 3,000 of the limited-edition model for customers. Naturally the CVO Road Glide model bore the same chassis improvements that Harley-Davidson gave the entire FL line that year. An all-new frame coupled with better suspension settings produced a taut ride and snappier steering and handling through turns. Of course, the CVO Road Glide model dripped with excess, too. Like all CVO models, its accessory list was staggering and included countless chrome items, the Rumble Collection of hand and foot controls, Blade wheels, and a Harman/Kardon Advanced Audio System with AM/FM receiver and CD/MP3 player. All CVO models that year also included unique ignition keys and indoor bike covers with embroidered CVO logos.

SPECIFICATIONS

Engine Displacement:	110 cubic inches
Weight:	847 pounds
Seat Height:	26.3 inches
MSRP:	$30,999

LORE

- The 2000 Road Glide was the first CVO model to display the distinctive Screamin' Eagle graphics.
- The most expensive CVO bike for 2009 was the Ultra Classic Electra-Glide model at $35,499.

2009 FXSTSSE CVO™ SOFTAIL® SPRINGER®

The 2009 CVO Softail Springer model took the Rocker model's swingarm and oil tank assembly and the Springer model's frame, along with a 240mm rear tire. Even though the fork design dates back more than seven decades, it serves up a compliant ride for CVO Softail Springer riders. Another feature found on the CVO Softail Springer model is the front and rear wheel combination. Rarely does Harley-Davidson put 18-inch diameter wheels front and rear on a motorcycle, but that's just what you'll find on this 2009 model: the front tire is a 130/70x18 and the rear is the massive 240/55x18. This started a trend for CVO models to come.

SPECIFICATIONS

Engine Displacement:	110 cubic inches
Weight:	752 pounds
Wheelbase:	65 inches
MSRP:	$26,999

LORE

- The CVO Softail Springer was the only model in Harley's entire fleet for 2009 using the classic fork.
- The 110B engine produced 110 lbs-ft of torque at 3000 rpm.

2010 CVO™ SOFTAIL® CONVERTIBLE

Harley-Davidson's 2010 Softail Convertible model transformed from a cross-country touring bike to cross-town custom cruiser simply by removing the quick-detach saddlebags and windscreen. The stylish bike was functional, providing comfortable long-distance riding. Among the new accessories that helped make the Softail Convertible were leather-covered saddlebags with genuine buffalo-hide inserts, a leather seat and detachable passenger pillion and backrest, a detachable fairing with smoke-tint windscreen, 18-inch chromed aluminum Stinger wheels with matching Stinger sprocket and brake rotors, lowered rear suspension, Rumble Collection foot and hand controls, and the Twin Cam 110B engine. The Softail Convertible model carried an MSRP of $27,999.

SPECIFICATIONS

Engine Displacement:	110 cubic inches
Weight:	724 pounds
Wheelbase:	64.2 inches
Seat Height:	24.4 inches

LORE

- *Thunder Press* reported: "Like every CVO creation, the Convertible is accessorized with an exhaustive list of custom components, components that are rarely there for practical purposes."

- *Motorcyclist* magazine reported about the Convertible: "The quick-change windshield and bags actually change quite quickly once you master the drill."

2010 CVO™ ELECTRA-GLIDE® ULTRA CLASSIC

With an MSRP of $35,999, the CVO Electra-Glide Ultra Classic model is among the most expensive Harley-Davidsons ever built. But a customer gets a lot of bang for the buck—figuratively and literally. The 110-cubic-inch engine produces 115 lbs-ft of torque, and the sum of the CVO Ultra Classic's parts would cost much more to duplicate if a customer were to buy the components individually and place them on a new bike. Moreover, the CVO models are produced in limited quantities, so they often hold their value longer than their standard counterparts. So what are among the standard features that a customer gets with the CVO Ultra Classic model? The 110-inch engine and a bevy of other Screamin' Eagle performance parts, custom wheels and matching foot and hand controls, heated hand grips, anti-lock brakes, an 80-watt sound system, and plenty of chromed and polished parts. And, to further set it from other Electra-Glide models, the CVO bike's paint scheme includes flame graphics that run from front to back. Membership clearly has its privileges.

SPECIFICATIONS

Engine Displacement:	110 cubic inches
Wheels:	17 inch front, 16 inch rear
Weight:	887 pounds
Seat Height:	27.4 inches

LORE

- The CVO line debuted in 1999.
- Only four CVO models are produced each year, all in limited numbers.

2011 CVO™ STREET GLIDE®

"The best of the best" pretty much sums up the 2011 CVO Street Glide model, because even in standard form the FLHX Street Glide is one of Harley-Davidson's top-selling models. It was a sure bet as a CVO model, too, which explains why the Motor Company offered 3,700 of them for 2011, each with an MSRP of $32,499. Interestingly, in the process of developing the CVO Street Glide, the touring model originally predicated on less chrome and fewer accessories got more chrome parts and bolt-on components included in the package. While the CVO Street Glide model lacks the bulbous Tour-Pak travel trunk, it was given a set of ventilated fairing lowers and engine guard bars, plus a passenger backrest, giving the bike more of a weighted-down look than before. But a restyled front fender with accompanying seven-spoke 19-inch Agitator wheel makes it clear to viewers that this is no ordinary touring bike. Helping improve the ride are adjustable rear shock absorbers, and for listening enjoyment, the six-speaker sound system is powered by a 100-watt-per-channel amplifier. Like all CVO models, the Street Glide is finished in a striking paint job; four color combinations were available.

SPECIFICATIONS

Engine Displacement:	110 cubic inches
Weight:	814 pounds
Seat Height:	27.4 inches
Tires:	130/60x19 front, 180/55x18 rear

LORE

• The CVO Street Glide bike's 19-inch front wheel is the largest ever for a Harley-Davidson touring model.

• The CVO Street Glide's smoke-tint windscreen is slightly taller than the standard model's windscreen.

2013 CVO BREAK OUT

Slammed and chopped style goes premium in the all-new CVO™ Break Out. Custom details abound on this machine, from the chopped front fender and turbine-styled hub attached to the lowered and raked front fork to the one-piece forged aluminum supports holding the bobbed rear fender to the frame. Hand-polished metal paint with lace effects take the high standard set by CVO paint to even greater heights. All the quality. All the legacy of the Harley-Davidson name. Plus custom touches and performance that distinguish you from every other bike on the road. Sure there's a little vanity. Premium custom. Big, tricked-out wheels. Deep attention to details. The perfect storm of engineering and style you'll only find on a custom machine. And you'll spoil yourself with the accessories—from comfort to electronics to chrome. But the real signature of a Harley-Davidson® Custom Vehicle Operations™ motorcycle is the explosive power and sleek detailing of the huge Twin Cam 110™ with Screamin' Eagle® engine badges. It's custom-built, not just for anyone, but for true connoisseurs of the road.

SPECIFICATIONS

Price:	$26,499
Length:	96.3 inches
Seat Height:	24.8 inches
Wheelbase:	67.3 inches

LORE

- The original CVO Breakout had one of the most outrageous custom paint jobs ever offered on a production motorcycle.

- The Breakout captured the style of one-off custom motorcycles in a (limited) production model.

PHOTOGRAPHER'S NOTES

BY DAVID BLATTEL

My career as a professional photographer began when I opened my first commercial studio in 1978. From the start, one of my fantasies was to shoot for the Harley-Davidson Motor Company. In 1989, that dream came true when I was chosen to shoot for their calendar. It was a major production with big interior sets, beautiful models, and a good-size crew. It was a lot of hard work, but I loved every minute of it! I shot that calendar for Harley-Davidson for five fun years, and I haven't stopped shooting Harley-Davidson motorcycles since.

Back then I shot with a 4x5-view camera, the kind where you put a black cloth over your head to view the ground glass from the rear to focus and compose and then inserted a sheet film holder before every photo was taken—not much different from the cameras used in the early days of photography. By 2003, I was shooting bikes on medium format 2¼ x 2¾ transparency film, using a Mamiya RZ67 camera. In 2005, I purchased the first 35mm full sensor digital camera, a 16-megapixel 35mm Canon 1dsMkII. The digital quality was amazing, every bit as good as film, and in many ways superior.

With the transition from large format, to medium format, then to 35mm digital, I'd built quite an archive through the years. Each year I locate new model bikes I want to shoot through dealerships and seek out vintage bikes through private collectors. Once I've located the bikes I'm interested in photographing, the location scouting begins.

Location scouting is a very personal experience for me, and each location has to fit that particular bike. Some locations come pretty easy; others drive me nuts. I can feel when I find the right location; something inside me tells me that the bike and location match. Each and every year, I've been amazed at the locations I come up with and the exceptional cooperation I receive from the landowners and businesses that allow me to photograph on their properties. I can't thank enough all the bike collectors, dealerships, location providers, and assistants who have helped me out over the years. I couldn't have created these shots without them.

Once I coordinate the location and the bike and the time of day I need to shoot, the production begins. Some locations require minimal lighting, where I'm generally waiting to shoot right when the sun is setting or right after it goes below the horizon. Other times I have to light the entire scene, which of course requires more time to set up and test lighting while still being ready for the right natural light, if that's also in the shot.

I like working with a small crew, usually a couple of assistants and me. The owners often stick around for the vintage bike shoots. With new bikes, the dealerships generally drop off the bikes and I give them an estimated pickup time.

Because of my experience shooting bikes, I need them only for a short period, anywhere from two to four hours. But if I know there may be logistical problems, I'll take whatever lead time is necessary to ensure I'll get the shot.

Having shot Harley-Davidson's for so many years, and since I'm usually the one who's moving the bikes, I may have pushed bikes more distance than I've ridden them.

When Motorbooks editor Darwin Holmstrom approached me last year with the idea of publishing a collection of my photography under the title *Art of the Harley-Davidson Motorcycle*, I was more than excited—ecstatic is probably a better word. To have all of these Harley-Davidson photographs in one collaborative work goes beyond my original fantasy from some 33 years ago. I'd like to thank Darwin for all the support on this and the many other projects we've done together since our first association in 2003. Thanks also to the designers and printers who've taken care in the presentation of my photography.

—David Blattel,
Topanga, California, 2011

OWNER CREDITS

Includes restoration (res) details, page numbers in bold type: *Cover and front endpaper* 2009 FXDFSE CVO Fat Bob, courtesy J.C. Little, Harley Davidson Anaheim-Fullerton; *Title page* 1941 Model FL, Landy Brakke; **5** 1928 Model JDH, Alex Bella, courtesy of Bator International; **11** 1911 Model 7 Single, The Gilbert Family; **12** 1915 Model 11-F, Ronald Paugh; **15** 1915 Model 11-J with Sidecar, Nace Panzica; **16** 1918 Model 18-J, George Pardos, res Mike Parti; **17** 1926 Model BA, Mike Parti (and res); **19** 1927 Model JDS with Sidecar, Jay Leno; **20** 1928 Model JDH, Michael Thompson; **23** 1932 Model VL, Jay Leno; **24** 1933 Model VLD, Nace Panzica, location courtesy Virginia & Truckee Railroad, Virginia City, Nevada; **26** 1934 Model VLD, Carson Little; **27** 1937 Model UL, Jim Frankel; **29** 1940 Model UL, John Messina, res Paul Wheeler; **30** 1942 Model WLA, Paul Wheeler (and res); **33** 1951 Model G Servi-Car, Jim Frankel; **35** 1936 Model EL, Glen Bator/Bator International; **36** 1941 Model FL, Chuck Vogel, res Paul Whitehurst, 1941 Stearman PT-17 courtesy of Rich Ferdon; **39** 1946 Model EL, Phil Jennemann; **40** 1947 Model EL, Louie Fisher; **43** 1947 Model FL Police, Paul Wheeler (and res); **45** 1949 Model FL, Rob Steckel, res Paul Wheeler; **46** 1952 Model FL, Frank Roque; **48** 1954 Model FLF Police Bike, Paul Wheeler (and res); **49** 1956 Model FL, Paul Wheeler (and res); **51** 1956 Model FLHF, "Panhead" Jimmy Detrick; **52** 1960 Model FL, Paul Wheeler (and res); **55** 1963 Model FLH, Michael Thompson; **56** 1964 Model FL, Ron Paugh (green & white); **59** 1955 Model ST, Paul Wheeler (and res); **60** 1956 Model KH, Ty Threedouble, Threedouble Family; **63** 1963 Model BTH Scat, Chea Zevnick; **64** 1995 MT500, Matthew Davis, location courtesy Maynard Station, Silver City Nevada; **67** 1963 Sportster XLCH, Vinnie Mandzak; **68** 1972 Sportster, Steve Hana; **71** 1977 XLCR Sportster, Steve Hana; **72** 1984 XR1000, Vinnie Mandzak, courtesy Peterson Museum; **75** 2004 Sportster Roadster, Tom Scott, courtesy of Harley-Davidson Anaheim-Fullerton; **76** 2005 Sportster 883 Custom, courtesy Brian Scott/Harley-Davidson Anaheim-Fullerton; **77** 2006 XL883R Sportster, courtesy Jan Williams/Ventura Harley-Davidson; **78** 2007 XL 883L Sportster 883 Low, courtesy of Tim Lach, Kauai Harley-Davidson, Hawaii, Transportation & Prep, Chris Kurz and "da crew"; **81** 2008 XL1200N Nightster, courtesy of Noah Von Doeren/Ventura Harley-Davidson; **82** 2009 XL1200C Sportster 1200 Custom, courtesy of Forrest Nolin, Bartels' Harley-Davidson; **85** 2010 Sportster XR-1200, courtesy, Tracey Warriner/Ventura Harley-Davidson; **86** 2011 Forty-Eight Sportster, Randy and Frannie Oligo and Kauai Harley-Davidson; **89** 1966 Electra-Glide Shovelhead, John Sanderson, res Paul Wheeler; **90** 1966 Nevada Highway Patrol, Ron Paugh; **93** 1967 FLH Electra-Glide (1966), Robert C. Foster, courtesy of Brian Miller, res Paul Wheeler; **94** 1967 FLH Electra-Glide Police Model, Paul Wheeler (and res); **97** 1968 Model FLHFB Electra-Glide, Louie Fisher; **98** 1977 FLH Electra-Glide, Rob Steckel; **101** 1980 FLH Electra-Glide, Dean Shawler; **102** 2003 Ultra Classic Electra-Glide, Mark McCaw; **103** 2005 Road King Custom, courtesy Brian Scott/Harley-Davidson of Anaheim-Fullerton; **104** 2005 Road Glide, courtesy J.C. Little/Harley-Davidson of Anaheim-Fullerton; **107** 2006 FLHXI Street Glide, courtesy Brian Scott/Harley-Davidson Anaheim-Fullerton; **108** 2007 FLHR Road King Firefighter Special Edition, Steve Heller, New York Fire Truck, courtesy owner,

Mark W. Platt, originally from Engine Company 323 of Lawrence Cedar Hurst Station; **110** 2007 FLTR Road Glide, courtesy Tim Lach, Kauai Harley-Davidson, Hawaii, Transportation & Prep, Chris Kurz and "da crew"; **111** 2009 FLHX Street Glide, courtesy of Jan Williams/Ventura Harley-Davidson; **112** 2010 Road Glide Custom, courtesy of Golden Gate H-D; **115** 2010 Street Glide Trike, courtesy Jan Williams/Ventura Harley-Davidson; **116** 2011 Road King, courtesy Lester Veik/Skip Fordyce Harley-Davidson, riverside location courtesy Tilden Coil Constructors; **119** 1977 FX Low Rider, Oliver Shokouh/Harley-Davidson of Glendale; **120** 1980 Model FXWG-80 Wide Glide, Ronald Paugh/Paughco **123** 2006 FXDI35 35th Anniversary Super Glide, courtesy J.C. Little/Harley-Davidson of Anaheim-Fullerton; **124** 2006 FXDBI Dyna Street Bob, courtesy Brian Scott/Fullerton Harley-Davidson; **127** 2008 FXDF Fat Bob, courtesy Jan Williams/Ventura Harley-Davidson; **128** 2008 FXDC Dyna Super Glide Custom, courtesy Tracey Warriner/Ventura Harley-Davidson; **131** 2010 Dyna Wide Glide, Gretta Boyd; **133** 1985 Model FXST Softail, Bob Caldwell; **134** 2005 Softail Springer Classic, courtesy Allan Frank/Los Angeles Harley-Davidson; **137** 2006 FXSTI Softail Standard, courtesy Jan Williams/Ventura Harley-Davidson; **138** 2007 FLSTN Softail Deluxe, courtesy Brian Scott/Harley-Davidson Anaheim-Fullerton; **141** 2008 FXCW Rocker C, courtesy Allan Frank/Los Angeles Harley-Davidson; **142** 2008 FLSTSB Softail Cross Bones, courtesy Jan Williams/Ventura Harley-Davidson; **145** 2010 Fat Boy Lo, courtesy Tracey Warriner/Ventura Harley-Davidson; **146** 2011 Heritage Softail Classic, courtesy Jan Williams/Ventura Harley-Davidson, location courtesy Oxnard Pallet; **149** 2011 Softail Deluxe, courtesy Lester Veik/Skip Fordyce Harley-Davidson, riverside location courtesy Tilden Coil Constructors; **151** 1921 Model 221 8-Valve Racer, M. F. Egan; **152** 1924 8-Valve Racer, The Gilbert Family; **153** WR Racer, Jay Leno; **154** KRTT, The Gilbert Family; **157** 1977 MX 250, Oliver Shokouh/Harley-Davidson of Glendale; **158** 2006 V-Rod Destroyer, Tim Lach and Kauai Harley-Davidson; **161** 2003 V-Rod, Jay Leno; **162** 2005 V-Rod, courtesy J.C. Little/Harley-Davidson Anaheim-Fullerton; **165** 2006 VRSCR Street Rod, courtesy Jan Williams Ventura Harley-Davidson; **166** 2007 VRSDX Night Rod Special, Rocco Maramonte; **169** 2009 VRSCF V-Rod Muscle, courtesy Forrest Nolin, Bartels' Harley-Davidson; **170** 2011 Night Rod Special, thanks to Rusty & Josh, Pomona Valley Harley-Davidson; **173** 2002 FLHRSET Screamin' Eagle CVO Road King, courtesy J.C. Little/Harley-Davidson Anaheim-Fullerton; **174** 2007 FXSTSSE Screamin' Eagle CVO Softail Springer, courtesy Brian Scott, Harley Davidson Anaheim-Fullerton; **177** 2008 FXDSE2 Screamin' Eagle CVO Dyna, courtesy Forrest Nolin, Bartels, Harley-Davidson; **178** 2008 FLHRSE4 Screamin' Eagle Road King, courtesy Tracey Warriner/Ventura Harley-Davidson; **181** 2009 FLTRSE CVO Road Glide, Greg Khougaz; **182** 2009 FXSTSSE CVO Softail Springer, Gordon Capel; **183** 2010 CVO Softail Convertible, courtesy Brian Scott, Harley Davidson Anaheim-Fullerton; **185** 2010 CVO Electra-Glide Ultra Classic, courtesy J.C. Little, Harley Davidson Anaheim-Fullerton; **186** 2011 CVO Street Glide, "J-Boy" Smith and Kauai Harley-Davidson; **189** 1946 Model FL, Phil Jennemann; *Opposite* 2011 Dyna Super Glide Custom, courtesy Jan Williams, Ventura Harley-Davidson.

INDEX